THE
100+
SERIES™

Reproducible Activities

Mixed Skills in Math

Keeping Students Sharp With Daily Practice and Review

Grades 5-6

By
Jillayne Prince Wallaker

Instructional Fair
An imprint of Carson-Dellosa Publishing LLC
Greensboro, North Carolina

Instructional Fair

Author: Jillayne Prince Wallaker
Editors: Elizabeth Flikkema, Wendy Roh Jenks, Linda Triemstra
Cover Artist: Corel Corporation
Interior Artist: Becky Radtke

Instructional Fair
An imprint of Carson-Dellosa Publishing LLC
PO Box 35665
Greensboro, NC 27425 USA

ISBN 978-1-56822-860-0
091118091

Table of Contents

Name _____

▲ Add.

1.
$$45{,}367$$
$$+\ 6{,}254$$
$$\overline{51{,}621}$$

2.
$$52{,}168$$
$$+28{,}931$$
$$\overline{80{,}099}$$

3.
$$16{,}280$$
$$+70{,}942$$
$$\overline{87{,}222}$$

4.
$$6{,}238$$
$$+85{,}399$$
$$\overline{91{,}637}$$

5.
$$70{,}471$$
$$+\ 46{,}055$$
$$\overline{116526}$$

6.
$$28{,}633$$
$$+\ 7{,}468$$
$$\overline{36{,}101}$$

7.
$$8{,}900$$
$$+\ 14{,}152$$
$$\overline{23{,}052}$$

8.
$$39{,}295$$
$$+\ 16{,}297$$
$$\overline{55{,}592}$$

▲ Write the numeral for each number word.

1. Six hundred thousand, four _600,004_

2. Forty-five billion, eight million, seventy-three thousand, one hundred five

   _____

3. Two hundred sixty million, four hundred fifty-one thousand _____

4. Nine hundred billion, one thousand, eighty-two _____

5. Three hundred ninety-five million, seven hundred sixty thousand, eight hundred thirty-six

   _____

▲ Write the first ten multiples other than zero of 4, 7, and 9.

4	**8**	12	16	20	24	28	32	36	40
7	14	21	28	35	42	49	56	63	70
9	18	27	36	45	54				
	63	72	81	90					

Bonus Box: Draw or stamp five different ways to make $1.45 using coins.

Name _____

▲ Subtract.

1.
  82,461
– 35,372
  47,089

2.
  64,228
– 51,379
  12,849

3.
  55,724
–38,265
  17,459

4.
  37,510
– 9,362
  28,148

5.
  70,534
–46,055

6.
  28,633
– 8,924

7.
  94,631
– 17,445

8.
  64,505
– 21,746

▲ Write the numeral for each number word.

1. Twenty-six billion, fifty million, one hundred thirty-five thousand, eight hundred forty-seven

   _____

2. Two million, sixty-nine thousand, one _____

3. Five hundred billion, forty-four _____

4. One hundred eighty-two thousand _____

5. Seventy-six million, eight hundred twenty-seven thousand, five hundred thirty-nine

   _____

▲ Write the first ten multiples other than zero of 3, 5, and 8.

   __3__ ____ ____ ____ ____ ____ ____ ____ ____ ____ ____

   __5__ ____ ____ ____ ____ ____ ____ ____ ____ ____ ____

   __8__ ____ ____ ____ ____ ____ ____ ____

   ____ ____ ____ ____

Bonus Box: Choose five of the above subtraction problems and use addition to check your answers.

6

▲ Add or subtract.

1.
```
   36,739
+  69,331
```

2.
```
   68,472
+  16,559
```

3.
```
   70,331
-  46,935
```

4.
```
   28,633
-   9,468
```

5.
```
   72,280
-  18,942
```

6.
```
    7,489
+  69,043
```

7.
```
   14,863
+  46,456
```

8.
```
   46,835
+  22,886
```

▲ Write each set of numbers in order from least to greatest.

1. 9,567,342   _____

9,567,432   _____

9,557,442   _____

2. 5,768,209,472   _____

5,756,209,472   _____

5,760,209,472   _____

3. 800,306,101,002   _____

800,036,101,002   _____

800,306,011,002   _____

▲ Write the first ten multiples other than zero of 3 and 4.

__3__ ____ ____ ____ ____ ____ ____ ____ ____ ____ ____

__4__ ____ ____ ____ ____ ____ ____ ____ ____ ____ ____

Name two common multiples of 3 and 4. _____ _____

What is the least common multiple (LCM) of 3 and 4? _____

Bonus Box: Choose an addition or subtraction problem from the top of the page. Write a story problem to illustrate it.

Name _____

▲ Add or subtract.

1.
62,437
− 28,952

2.
53,299
+ 37,363

3.
46,783
+ 48,946

4.
72,304
− 56,285

5.
67,442
− 28,617

6.
44,381
− 7,845

7.
48,968
+ 17,593

8.
86,235
− 39,361

▲ Write each set of numbers in order from least to greatest.

1. 798,567,330   _____
   798,576,330   _____
   798,567,303   _____

2. 8,960,783,006   _____
   8,966,783,006   _____
   8,906,783,006   _____

3. 67,340,806,151 _____
   67,340,806,115 _____
   67,304,806,115 _____

▲ Write the first ten multiples other than zero of 6 and 8.

   6 ___ ___ ___ ___ ___ ___ ___ ___ ___ ___

   8 ___ ___ ___ ___ ___ ___ ___ ___ ___ ___

Name two common multiples of 6 and 8. _____ _____

What is the least common multiple (LCM) of 6 and 8? _____

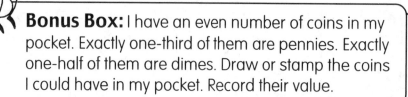

Bonus Box: I have an even number of coins in my pocket. Exactly one-third of them are pennies. Exactly one-half of them are dimes. Draw or stamp the coins I could have in my pocket. Record their value.

▲ Add.

1.
```
  5,352,304
    621,784
     75,928
      9,060
+       331
```

2.
```
    257,351
    345,103
    463,829
     34,615
+    16,429
```

3.
```
  6,072,580
  1,638,227
    410,300
      5,788
+       942
```

4.
```
    553,047
    260,042
     38,452
      4,276
+       743
```

5.
```
     71,331
     25,638
     40,205
     60,873
+     9,735
```

6.
```
  4,528,633
    476,229
    313,531
    145,003
+    23,068
```

▲ Round . . .

1. to the nearest ten thousand.

9,468,354   79,850,621,995   64,219,003

_____   _____   _____

2. to the nearest hundred million.

301,426,999   26,081,116,746   723,310,577,025

_____   _____   _____

3. to the nearest ten.

834,290,776,359   57,831,421   268,629,893,115

_____   _____   _____

▲ Write the LCM for each set of numbers.

1. 6 and 9 _____   **2.** 7 and 2 _____

3. 8 and 3 _____   **4.** 5 and 4 _____

5. 2 and 9 _____   **6.** 9 and 3 _____

Bonus Box: Write an even number that has seven digits. The sum of the digits is 5.

Name _____

▲ Add.

1.
```
  7,432,612
    325,544
     25,951
      4,276
+       507
```

2.
```
    480,902
    563,786
     64,299
     55,097
+    3,389
```

3.
```
  3,700,984
  2,735,546
     89,700
        658
+        79
```

4.
```
  1,235,536
    746,920
     67,322
      8,396
+     4,229
```

5.
```
    271,441
    156,362
     33,008
     70,485
+     6,766
```

6.
```
    618,633
    482,349
    386,574
     80,030
+    14,816
```

▲ Round . . .

1. to the nearest hundred.

45,636,665   21,290,093,413   6,452

_____   _____   _____

2. to the nearest ten billion.

301,438,426,999   598,234,510,097   744,967,799,960

_____   _____   _____

3. to the nearest hundred thousand.

45,002,961,504   567,738,892,035   4,521,892

_____   _____   _____

▲ Write the LCM for each set of numbers.

1. 7 and 4 _____   **2.** 3, 6, and 8 _____

3. 4, 6, and 9 _____   **4.** 2, 4, and 7 _____

5. 3, 4, and 6 _____   **6.** 2, 5, and 9 _____

Bonus Box: Write four numbers that when rounded to the nearest thousand, round to 456,000. Be sure to include numbers that round up and numbers that round down.

10

▲ Add.

1.
```
   486,685
   667,936
    45,733
     4,613
 +   6,745
```

2.
```
 7,475,923
    84,928
    68,641
       843
 +     677
```

3.
```
 1,472,895
 2,634,253
     5,963
     8,658
 +   6,379
```

4.
```
 4,121,614
   216,473
   112,532
    32,116
 +     829
```

5.
```
 1,736,253
 6,739,742
   759,052
    35,253
 +  89,005
```

6.
```
 6,754,386
   947,375
    67,732
     4,657
 +   6,731
```

▲ Round . . .

1. to the nearest ten.

674,476,352,226   30,800,562   253,499

_____   _____   _____

2. to the nearest hundred thousand.

34,562,748,445   147,823,463,455   321,233,425

_____   _____   _____

3. to the nearest hundred billion.

178,657,345,335   795,100,023,004   315,299,746,478

_____   _____   _____

▲ Write the numeral for each number word.

1. One million, forty-two thousand, three hundred

_____

2. Two hundred seventy-five billion, three

_____

Bonus Box: Find and list at least five things that occur in sets of 3.

▲ Subtract.

1.
452,567
– 154,859

2.
532,112
– 254,264

3.
724,324
– 152,578

4.
246,132
– 58,394

5.
703,523
– 612,408

6.
923,811
– 74,426

7.
823,645
– 541,773

8.
432,363
– 153,856

▲ Use front-end estimation to estimate each sum.
The first one is done for you.

1.
463   **500**
+ 218   **+ 200**
           700

2.
290
+ 472

3.
182
+ 563

4.
54,285
+ 32,687

5.
4,621
+ 1,532

6.
34,625
+ 37,543

7.
3,674
+ 4,463

8.
2,754
+ 4,343

▲ Write each set of numbers in order from least to greatest.

1. 465,543,376 _____
465,453,367 _____
465,543,367 _____

2. 790,574,400,503 _____
790,547,400,503 _____
709,547,400,503 _____

3. 20,593,557,408 _____
20,593,575,408 _____
20,593,557,480 _____

Bonus Box: Write four
five-digit numbers whose
digits have a sum of 8.

▲ Subtract.

1.
35,452,567
− 6,744,859

2.
11,253,645
− 6,745,365

3.
62,703,523
− 61,367,863

4.
73,623,811
−72,896,424

5.
90,464,766
− 1,526,899

6.
37,564,366
− 19,578,897

7.
4,532,067
− 2,541,773

8.
93,432,363
− 64,674,274

▲ Use front-end estimation to estimate each sum. The first one is done for you.

1.
743   **700**
+ 632 **+ 600**
       1,300

2.
583,639
+ 162,265

3.
3,673
+ 2,415

4.
314,526
+ 415,515

5.
3,425
+ 2,397

6.
45,632
+ 18,536

7.
7,221
+ 1,186

8.
473
+ 365

9.
8,345
+ 1,623

▲ Write the LCM for each set of numbers.

1. 5 and 9 _____
2. 2 and 3 _____
3. 6 and 9 _____
4. 3, 5, and 6 _____
5. 3, 6, and 15 _____
6. 4, 6, and 7 _____
7. 4, 6, and 10 _____
8. 2, 3, and 12 _____

Bonus Box: Choose five of the above subtraction problems and use addition to check your answers.

Name _____

▲ Subtract.

1.
```
  600,000
-  44,859
```

2.
```
 10,000,000
- 5,210,987
```

3.
```
  900,000
- 526,899
```

4.
```
  70,000,000
- 57,364,325
```

5.
```
 20,000,000
-  1,369,853
```

6.
```
 50,000,000
- 32,821,424
```

7.
```
 40,000,000
- 22,541,336
```

8.
```
 9,000,000
- 2,674,274
```

▲ Multiply.

1.
```
   8
 x 4
```

2.
```
   6
 x 7
```

3.
```
   5
 x 9
```

4.
```
   9
 x 8
```

5.
```
   2
 x 7
```

6.
```
   7
 x 7
```

7.
```
   9
 x 6
```

8.
```
   4
 x 7
```

9.
```
   8
 x 8
```

10.
```
   8
 x 3
```

▲ Round . . . .

1. to the nearest ten million.

45,839,208,211   672,899,905   5,398,210,647

_____   _____   _____

2. to the nearest hundred.

56,382,019   674,291,108,223   674,892

_____   _____   _____

3. to the nearest thousand.

633,298,987,028   62,165,119,624

_____   _____

Bonus Box: Choose one subtraction and two multiplication problems from this page. Write a story problem for each.

Name _____

▲ Subtract.

1.
  70,030
– 54,269

2.
  80,020,000
– 31,210,658

3.
  2,001,100
– 1,524,838

4.
  400,000
– 361,865

5.
  90,005,000
– 41,731,852

6.
  1,026,000
– 215,469

7.
  600,010
– 422,541

8.
  30,600,400
– 18,654,417

▲ Multiply.

1. 6 x 8 = _____   **2.** 5 x 7 = _____

3. 6 x 6 = _____   **4.** 9 x 8 = _____

5. 9 x 3 = _____   **6.** 3 x 6 = _____

7. 7 x 8 = _____   **8.** 5 x 8 = _____

9. 7 x 9 = _____   **10.** 2 x 8 = _____

11. 7 x 6 = _____   **12.** 9 x 4 = _____

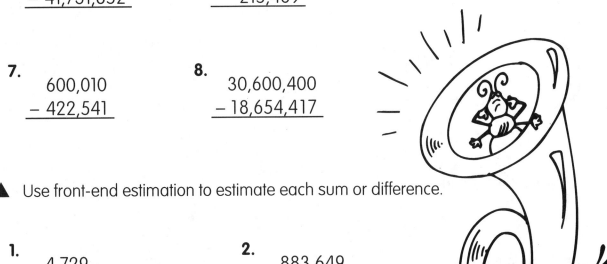

▲ Use front-end estimation to estimate each sum or difference.

1.
  4,729
+ 1,099

2.
  883,649
– 462,265

3.
  526,362
+ 215,875

4.
  28,425
+ 50,397

5.
  845,632
– 186,536

6.
  5,673
– 2,415

Bonus Box: Write ten number sentences, each with an answer of 65. Be sure to include addition, subtraction, multiplication, and division problems.

IF87123 • Mixed Skills in Math 5-6

Name _____

▲ Subtract.

1.
  45,890,000
– 21,564,269

2.
  17,300,542
–10,658,839

3.
  893,001
– 396,273

4.
  9,000,120
– 728,203

5.
  80,000,000
– 61,173,862

6.
  98,500,300
– 21,785,469

7.
  320,001
– 102,546

8.
  60,004,100
– 14,085,307

▲ Record the perimeter.

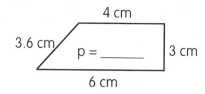

4 cm / 6 cm / p = _____

6 cm / 4 cm / p = _____ / 3 cm / 2 cm

4 cm / 3.6 cm / p = _____ / 3 cm / 6 cm

▲ Write the numeral for each number word.

1. One hundred billion, ten million, two thousand, sixty-nine _____

2. Seven hundred thirty-five thousand, three _____

3. Six billion, one million, five _____

4. Two hundred ten million, sixty-four thousand _____

Bonus Box: Write six numbers that when rounded to the nearest ten million, round to 8,450,000,000. Be sure to include numbers that round up and numbers that round down.

16

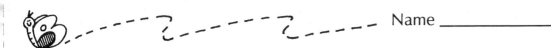
▲ On lined paper, arrange in columns and add. Write the sums here.

1. 242 + 67 + 85 + 463 + 689 + 58 + 147 + 38 = _____

2. 845 + 1,603 + 54 + 286 + 3,661 + 598 + 2,286 = _____

3. 861 + 99 + 38 + 5,484 + 27 + 6,310 + 77 + 184 = _____

4. 2,809 + 465 + 94 + 56,893 + 811 + 51,382 + 38 = _____

5. 273 + 574 + 29 + 36 + 6,382 + 43 + 7,386 + 48 + 82 = _____

▲ Label the Venn diagram.

_____ _____

▲ Multiply.

1. 6 x 6 = _____   **2.** 8 x 5 = _____

3. 9 x 4 = _____   **4.** 3 x 7 = _____

5. 5 x 9 = _____   **6.** 4 x 7 = _____

7. 6 x 9 = _____   **8.** 7 x 8 = _____

9. 8 x 9 = _____   **10.** 7 x 6 = _____

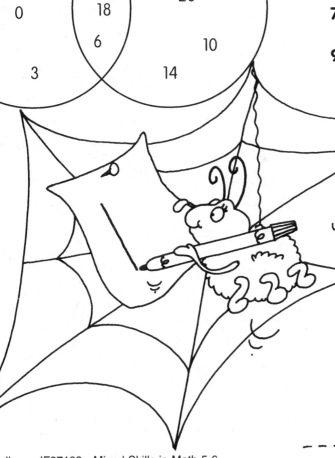

Bonus Box: Sketch a quadrilateral that is not a rectangle. Draw only two sides the same length. Measure each side and record the perimeter.

Name _____

▲ On lined paper, arrange in columns and add. Write the sums here.

1. 45,678 + 869 + 5,629 + 8,311 + 632 + 28 + 746 = _____

2. 667 + 3,845 + 62,327 + 162 + 45,362 + 3,522 + 73 = _____

3. 14,626 + 734 + 6,823 + 61,415 + 774 + 11,182 + 248 = _____

4. 6,272 + 118 + 926 + 21,721 + 62,006 + 704 + 2,781 = _____

5. 91 + 728 + 7,283 + 511 + 79 + 2,617 + 28,837 + 821 = _____

▲ Divide.

1. 24 ÷ 4 = _____   **2.** 36 ÷ 6 = _____

3. 42 ÷ 7 = _____   **4.** 45 ÷ 5 = _____

5. 48 ÷ 8 = _____   **6.** 63 ÷ 9 = _____

7. 49 ÷ 7 = _____   **8.** 72 ÷ 8 = _____

9. 27 ÷ 3 = _____   **10.** 28 ÷ 4 = _____

11. 25 ÷ 5 = _____   **12.** 35 ÷ 7 = _____

▲ Label the Venn diagram.

Bonus Box: Write four eight-digit odd numbers whose last six digits have a sum of ten.

_____ _____

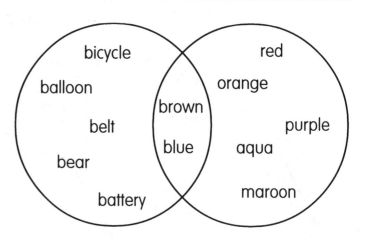

bicycle

balloon

belt

bear

battery

brown

blue

red

orange

purple

aqua

maroon

▲ On lined paper, arrange in columns and add. Write the sums here.

1. 789,256 + 765 + 1,245,789 + 87 + 804,277 + 485 = _____

2. 245 + 23,563,856 + 1,645 + 76,984,246 + 66 + 2,485 = _____

3. 65,287 + 123,352,118,089 + 69 + 325,456,983 + 286 = _____

4. 465,326,008 + 48 + 263,894 + 76,893,221 + 294,215,118 = _____

5. 76,839,456 + 123,782,093 + 35,689 + 54,389,256,891 = _____

▲ Divide.

1. $72 \div 8 =$ _____   **2.** $49 \div 7 =$ _____

3. $36 \div 4 =$ _____   **4.** $81 \div 9 =$ _____

5. $30 \div 6 =$ _____   **6.** $63 \div 9 =$ _____

7. $48 \div 6 =$ _____   **8.** $56 \div 8 =$ _____

9. $28 \div 4 =$ _____   **10.** $35 \div 7 =$ _____

11. $56 \div 7 =$ _____   **12.** $72 \div 9 =$ _____

▲ Write the LCM for each set of numbers.

1. 3, 6, and 11 _____

2. 4, 6, and 12 _____

3. 3, 6, and 7 _____

4. 6 and 12 _____

5. 3 and 13 _____

6. 6 and 9 _____

Bonus Box: I have six coins in my pocket. Their value is greater than 75¢ and less than $2.00. None of the coins is a quarter. Draw or stamp the coins I could have.

Name _____

▲ Add or subtract.

1.
```
  2,647,934
    363,829
     54,275
+    26,738
```

2.
```
  94,000,300
-  6,254,268
```

3.
```
  67,368,223
+ 25,524,938
```

4.
```
  42,671,003
  22,462,930
      67,364
+      3,991
```

5.
```
  80,400,020
- 57,034,227
```

6.
```
  70,000,100
- 21,485,469
```

7.
```
  30,042,100
- 12,761,042
```

8.
```
  63,097,620
+ 28,468,728
```

▲ Multiply or divide.

1. $49 \div 7 =$ _____   2. $7 \times 8 =$ _____

3. $8 \times 6 =$ _____   4. $9 \times 5 =$ _____

5. $9 \times 7 =$ _____   6. $32 \div 4 =$ _____

7. $36 \div 6 =$ _____   8. $6 \times 9 =$ _____

9. $6 \times 8 =$ _____   10. $4 \times 7 =$ _____

11. $81 \div 9 =$ _____   12. $42 \div 6 =$ _____

13. $5 \times 6 =$ _____   14. $56 \div 7 =$ _____

15. $8 \times 3 =$ _____   16. $7 \times 9 =$ _____

▲ Record the perimeter.

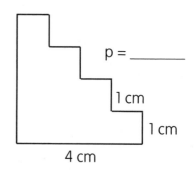

p = _____

1 cm

1 cm

4 cm

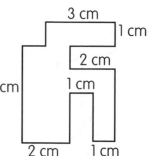

3 cm

1 cm

2 cm

4 cm

1 cm

2 cm   1 cm

p = _____

5 cm

3 cm

p = _____

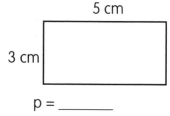

Bonus Box: Draw or stamp at least five ways to make $1.87 using coins.

Name _____

▲ Add or subtract.

1.
    90,002,610
  – 26,173,702

2.
    3,617,002
      702,835
       22,672
  +   6,358

3.
    57,893,020
  – 20,896,336

4.
    11,573,947
     9,987,101
     2,526,473
  +   453,728

5.
    72,182,346
  – 22,674,596

6.
    52,783,489
  + 19,145,734

7.
    60,000,000
  – 35,610,025

8.
    72,000,200
  – 41,836,634

▲ Use front-end estimation to estimate each sum or difference.

1.
    35,872
  – 21,543

2.
    377,800
  + 452,736

3.
      902
  –   534

4.
    7,639
  + 2,100

5.
    472,984
  – 119,897

6.
    54,377
  + 61,635

▲ Find the area.

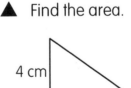

4 cm

6 cm

a = _____ cm²

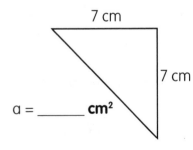

7 cm

7 cm

a = _____ cm²

6 cm

8 cm

a = _____ cm²

Bonus Box: Write six numbers that when rounded to the nearest hundred thousand, round to 34,600,000. Include numbers that round up and numbers that round down.

Name _____

▲ Multiply.

| 1. 36 x 20 | 2. 74 x 50 | 3. 28 x 60 | 4. 49 x 70 | 5. 53 x 40 |

| 6. 63 x 30 | 7. 82 x 70 | 8. 57 x 80 | 9. 36 x 10 | 10. 89 x 90 |

▲ Find the factors of each number using a factor tree. The first one shows you how.

1.

```
      84
     /  \
   12    7
  /  \
 6    2
/ \
3   2
```

2. 98

3. 24

4. 50

5. 189

6. 80

Find the greatest common factor (GCF) of 50 and 80. _____

▲ Multiply or divide.

1. 4 x 7 = _____   2. 36 ÷ 6 = _____   3. 48 ÷ 6 = _____

4. 9 x 6 = _____   5. 3 x 9 = _____   6. 5 x 8 = _____

7. 56 ÷ 7 = _____   8. 8 x 7 = _____   9. 64 ÷ 8 = _____

Bonus Box: Look around the room for objects with angles. Trace ten acute angles and label where you found them.

Name _____

▲ Multiply.

1. 40	2. 89	3. 17	4. 90	5. 60
x 32	x 50	x 30	x 40	x 75

6. 58	7. 63	8. 50	9. 78	10. 70
x 80	x 70	x 36	x 10	x 90

▲ Find the factors of each number using a factor tree.

1. 86   **2.** 54   **3.** 180

Find the greatest common factor (GCF) of 54 and 180. _____

▲ On lined paper, arrange in columns and add. Write the sums here.

1. 641 + 58 + 894 + 1,286 + 3,668 + 93 + 285 = _____

2. 51,733 + 39 + 296 + 774 + 80 + 26,008 + 207 + 46 = _____

3. 62 + 89 + 10,830 + 253 + 6,472 + 29 = _____

4. 508 + 2,649 + 829 + 48 + 72,405 + 68 = _____

Bonus Box: Look around the room for objects with angles. Trace ten obtuse angles and label where you found them.

Name _____

▲ Divide.

1.
$60\overline{)2,100}$

2.
$20\overline{)920}$

3.
$50\overline{)4,850}$

4.
$40\overline{)1,520}$

5.
$60\overline{)3,540}$

6.
$30\overline{)2,460}$

7.
$70\overline{)4,410}$

8.
$90\overline{)2,610}$

▲ Find the perimeter of each figure.

1.
87 ft.

36 ft.

_____ **ft.**

2.
24 ft.

12 ft.

29 ft.

43 ft.

17 ft.   _____ **ft.**

67 ft.

3.
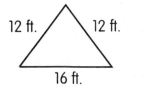
12 ft.   12 ft.

16 ft.

_____ **ft.**

4.
61 ft.

61 ft.   _____ **ft.**

5.

42 ft.

15 ft.

15 ft.

42 ft.

_____ **ft.**

▲ Write the greatest common factor (GCF) of each set of numbers.

48 and 12 _____   20 and 84 _____

32 and 18 _____   15 and 45 _____

82 and 144 _____   72 and 98 _____

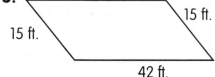

Bonus Box: Write ten equations with an answer of 66. Include addition, subtraction, multiplication, and division problems.

▲ Divide.

1.
60 ⟌ 1,920

2.
50 ⟌ 2,700

3.
80 ⟌ 1,680

4.
20 ⟌ 1,280

5.
90 ⟌ 1,260

6.
30 ⟌ 1,410

7.
70 ⟌ 5,110

8.
40 ⟌ 3,640

▲ Add or subtract.

1.
```
  40,070,000
− 16,273,372
```

2.
```
  72,102,324
− 46,192,455
```

3.
```
  57,893,020
  20,896,336
   6,499,021
+    577,283
```

4.
```
  28,904,544
   6,291,725
     873,928
+     90,762
```

▲ Find the perimeter of each figure.

1.
3 in.
5 in.   5 in.
_____ in.

2.
4 in.
12 in.
_____ in.

3.
10 in.
15 in.
8 in.   8 in.
_____ in.

4.
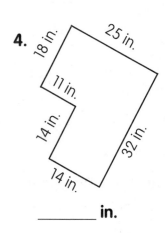
18 in.
25 in.
11 in.
14 in.
32 in.
14 in.
_____ in.

Bonus Box: Write six even numbers with seven digits each. The sum of the digits for each number is 15.

▲ Multiply or divide.

1.
32
x 60

2.
90 ⟌ 4,140

3.
89
x 30

4.
70 ⟌ 2,660

5.
46
x 50

6.
50 ⟌ 3,450

7.
77
x 40

8.
58
x 70

▲ Find the area of each figure.

1.
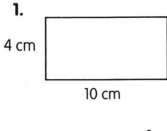
4 cm
10 cm

_____ cm²

2.
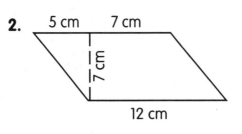
5 cm   7 cm
7 cm
12 cm

_____ cm²

3.
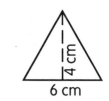
4 cm
6 cm

_____ cm²

▲ Find the perimeter of each figure.

1.
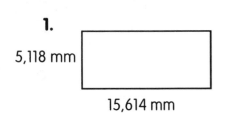
5,118 mm
15,614 mm

_____ mm

2.
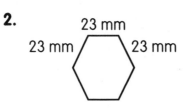
23 mm
23 mm   23 mm

_____ mm

3.
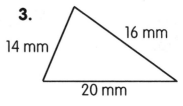
14 mm   16 mm
20 mm

_____ mm

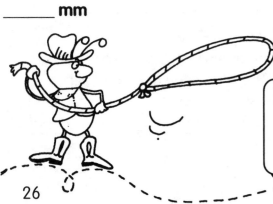

Bonus Box: Write six numbers that when rounded to the nearest ten million, round to 8,450,000,000. Be sure to include numbers that round up and numbers that round down.

▲ Multiply or divide.

1.
```
  57
x 20
```

2.
```
60 ) 2,280
```

3.
```
  93
x 60
```

4.
```
50 ) 2,350
```

5.
```
  99
x 40
```

6.
```
70 ) 6,160
```

7.
```
  39
x 90
```

8.
```
  24
x 60
```

▲ Find the area of each figure.

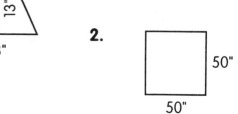

1. _____ in.²

13"
8"

2. _____ in.²

50"
50"

3. _____ in.²

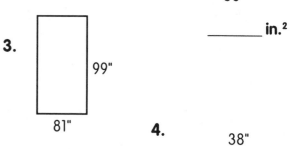

99"
81"

4. _____ in.²

38"
16"

5. _____ in.²

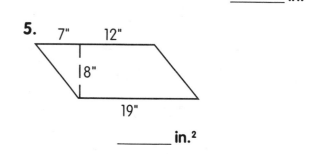

7"   12"
8"
19"

▲ Write the numeral for each number word.

1. Thirty billion, sixty-one thousand, eighty-eight _____

2. Six hundred million, twelve thousand, one hundred _____

3. Thirteen billion, two thousand, three _____

Bonus Box: Draw at least five ways to make $1.67 using coins.

Name _____

▲ Multiply.

1.	2.	3.	4.
52 x 13	21 x 68	13 x 23	43 x 22

5.	6.	7.	8.
14 x 12	31 x 39	72 x 14	33 x 31

▲ Round . . .

1. to the nearest tenth.

526.78   43,821.29   5,246.81

_____   _____   _____

2. to the nearest hundredth.

25.252   386.916   44,643.426

_____   _____   _____

3. to the nearest thousandth.

28.9215   567,543.2663   8.3647

_____   _____   _____

Bonus Box: Look around the room for objects with angles. Make a graph to show how many right, obtuse, and acute angles you find. Write two statements about your data.

▲ Find the perimeter of each figure.

1.

2,689 cm

2,689 cm ☐

_____ cm

2.

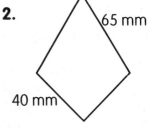

65 mm

40 mm

_____ mm

Name _____

▲ Multiply.

1.   26   2.   53   3.   42   4.   65
      x 41   x 62   x 74   x 51

5.   83   6.   62   7.   41   8.   80
      x 43   x 64   x 58   x 26

▲ Graph the following data about Yesenia's family vacation.

Number of Miles Traveled

Day	Miles
1	325
2	400
3–5	0
6	220
7	158
8	240
9	110

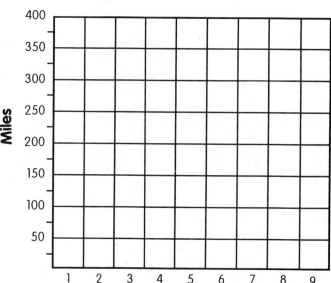

▲ Answer the following questions about the data.

1. How many miles did Yesenia's family travel in all? _____

2. How many miles did they travel on Day 6? _____

3. On which two consecutive days did they travel the farthest?

   _____   _____

4. Why do you think they didn't travel at all on days 3–5?

   _____

Bonus Box: Sketch two figures with perimeters of 36 units. Label the length of each side.

▲ Multiply.

1.
   47
   x 63

2.
   54
   x 36

3.
   27
   x 45

4.
   84
   x 19

5.
   37
   x 24

6.
   47
   x 65

7.
   78
   x 32

8.
   44
   x 65

▲ Write the numeral for each number word.

1. Three hundred five and twenty-five hundredths _____

2. Eight and one hundred forty-two thousandths _____

3. Two million, five and three hundred fifty-one thousandths _____

4. Five thousand and six hundredths _____

▲ Find the area of each figure.

1.
3 cm   15 cm
|10 cm
18 cm

_____ cm²

2.
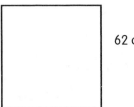
62 cm

62 cm

_____ cm²

3.
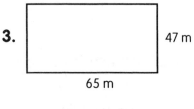
47 m
65 m

_____ m²

Bonus Box: Sketch two different rectangles with perimeters of 68 units. Label the length of each side. What is the area of each rectangle? Compare the areas and explain your answers.

Name _____

▲ Divide.

1.

23) 966

2.

41) 1,435

3.

64) 1,152

4.

53) 2,014

5.

67) 3,283

6.

72) 4,032

7.

38) 2,774

8.

97) 6,208

▲ Round . . .

1. to the nearest ten-thousandth.

5.62819921   46,829.00142366

_____   _____

2. to the nearest tenth.

6.8291234   6,829.394523

_____   _____

3. to the nearest hundredth.

52.73946   6.00923472957

_____   _____

▲ Write the numeral for each number word.

1. Twelve and fourteen thousandths

_____

2. Six thousand, one hundred and four hundredths

_____

3. Forty-five billion, seven thousand, six and five tenths

_____

4. Eight million, one thousand, ten and fifteen hundredths

_____

Bonus Box: Write the six rounded numbers in order from least to greatest.

Name _____

▲ Divide.

1.
$$45\overline{)1,035}$$

2.
$$27\overline{)2,322}$$

3.
$$53\overline{)2,173}$$

4.
$$67\overline{)1,206}$$

5.
$$32\overline{)3,104}$$

6.
$$58\overline{)3,596}$$

7.
$$76\overline{)4,028}$$

8.
$$41\overline{)1,394}$$

▲ Write each set of numbers in order from least to greatest.

1. 2,648.23145   _____

264.823145   _____

26,482.3145   _____

2. 6.198002   _____

6.19002   _____

6.189002   _____

3. 26.586102   _____

25.86102   _____

25.68102   _____

▲ Identify the length of **X** in each figure.

1.

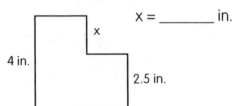

X = _____ in.

2.

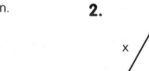

X = _____ in.

3.

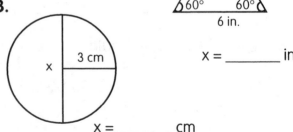

X = _____ cm

Bonus Box: Nine coins are in a bank. Exactly one-third are quarters. What could be the value of the coins in the bank? Illustrate two possibilities.

Name _____

▲ Divide.

1. $24\overline{)876}$

2. $47\overline{)2{,}894}$

3. $72\overline{)1{,}207}$

4. $53\overline{)2{,}260}$

5. $36\overline{)3{,}174}$

6. $69\overline{)1{,}838}$

7. $83\overline{)3{,}961}$

8. $15\overline{)708}$

▲ Write each set of numbers in order from least to greatest.

1. 4.675904 _____

　　46.75904 _____

　　4.657904 _____

2. 0.53442 _____

　　0.53424 _____

　　05.3442 _____

3. 367.38291 _____

　　36.738291 _____

　　36.378291 _____

▲ Write the least common multiple (LCM) for each set of numbers.

1. 2 and 7 _____

2. 4 and 10 _____

3. 6 and 8 _____

4. 5 and 3 _____

5. 11 and 3 _____

6. 10 and 6 _____

7. 12 and 6 _____

8. 5 and 2 _____

9. 6 and 9 _____

Bonus Box: Write an odd number that has 11 digits. The sum of the digits is 34.

Name _____

▲ Divide.

1.

34 ⟌ 409‾‾‾‾‾

2.

57 ⟌ 4,663‾‾‾‾‾

3.

12 ⟌ 1,168‾‾‾‾‾

4.

22 ⟌ 865‾‾‾‾‾

5.

72 ⟌ 1,797‾‾‾‾‾

6.

41 ⟌ 3,214‾‾‾‾‾

7.

99 ⟌ 5,612‾‾‾‾‾

8.

67 ⟌ 3,340‾‾‾‾‾

▲ Add.

1.
```
   58.864701
    7.152677
 +  9.38576
```

2.
```
    6,743.00921
      934.279488
 +  1,546.98032
```

3.
```
    158.53774
     45.627384
 +  5,821.27843
```

4.
```
   4,627.095054
     264.2723
 +      6.800989
```

▲ Write the numeral for each number word.

1. Three billion, forty-four and six hundredths _____

2. Four hundred sixty-eight thousandths _____

3. Three and two hundred five thousandths _____

Bonus Box: Find and list at least five things that come in sets of two.

Name _____

▲ Multiply or divide.

1.
```
   52
 x 67
```

2.
```
34 | 2,231
```

3.
```
15 | 723
```

4.
```
   71
 x 29
```

5.
```
48 | 1,694
```

6.
```
68 | 2,015
```

7.
```
   83
 x 59
```

8.
```
   37
 x 63
```

▲ Add.

1.
```
  463.900827
   54.82914
+2,473.241
```

2.
```
   7.920343
   3.22416
+ 63.786869
```

3.
```
 123.415266
  64.73786
+ 748.342756
```

4.
```
   5.487969
  43.65647
+ 2.6214658
```

▲ On lined paper, arrange in columns and add. Write the sums here.

1. 3,786 + 23 + 657 + 85 + 7,543 + 283 + 972 = _____

2. 78 + 354 + 62 + 4,536 + 3,270 + 84 + 28 + 99 + 31 = _____

3. 5,600 + 243 + 694 + 6,453 + 89 + 39 + 64 + 57 = _____

Bonus Box: Write ten number sentences with an answer of 0.125.

▲ Multiply or divide.

1. 47 ⟌ 2,740

2. 86 ⟌ 2,047

3.   64
       x 53

4.   39
       x 44

5.   78
       x 36

6. 32 ⟌ 2,657

7. 74 ⟌ 3,043

8.   21
       x 79

▲ Subtract.

1.
  632.52231
− 56.32743

2.
  54.622
− 32.8653

3.
  362.1106
− 170.26153

4.
  1.5672
− 0.834267

5.
  6.8
− 2.6437

6.
  1,674.21
− 547.446

▲ Write the greatest common factor (GCF) of each set of numbers.

1. 64 and 120 _____

2. 90 and 105 _____

3. 42 and 70 _____

4. 60 and 36 _____

5. 126 and 84 _____

6. 144 and 162 _____

Bonus Box: Sketch five different polygons. Assign each side a length and give the perimeter for each figure.

▲ Use the correct order of operations.

1. $4 \times (24 - 19) \div 2 + 3 =$ _____

2. $2 \times 6 - 21 \div 7 =$ _____

3. $25 \div 5 + 5 - (6 - 2) =$ _____

4. $100 \div (2 \times 6 - 2) =$ _____

5. $(6 + 8) \div 2 \times (4 - 1) =$ _____

6. $(4 + 5) \times (15 - 9) \div 2 =$ _____

7. $(8 + 4 \times 6) \div (9 + 7) =$ _____

8. $2 + 5 \times 3 + 16 \div 2 - 6 =$ _____

Bonus Box:
Change the parentheses from the order of operations problems to obtain the following different answers. Change number 4 to equal 200. Change number 5 to equal 30. Change number 8 to equal 23.

▲ Identify each solid.

1.   _____

2.   _____

3.   _____

4.   _____

5. _____

▲ Subtract.

1.
$$\begin{array}{r} 67.0098 \\ - \ 49.132 \\ \hline \end{array}$$

2.
$$\begin{array}{r} 72.1132 \\ - \ 25.32564 \\ \hline \end{array}$$

3.
$$\begin{array}{r} 7.20093 \\ - \ 1.324672 \\ \hline \end{array}$$

4.
$$\begin{array}{r} 2.6 \\ - \ 1.35214 \\ \hline \end{array}$$

5.
$$\begin{array}{r} 83.226 \\ - \ 16.00547 \\ \hline \end{array}$$

6.
$$\begin{array}{r} 264.36 \\ - \ 75.38311 \\ \hline \end{array}$$

▲ Use the correct order of operations.

1. $(3 + 6) \times 3 + 15 \div 5 =$ _____

2. $(2 \times 3 \times 10 + 4) \div (10 - 5 + 3) =$ _____

3. $2 \times (11 - 3) \div (14 - 6 \times 2) =$ _____

4. $8 \div 2 + (5 \times 3 - 5) \div 2 =$ _____

5. $1 \times 6 \div 3 + (20 - 2 \times 7) =$ _____

6. $(16 + 8 \div 2) \div (6 - 12 \div 6) =$ _____

7. $7 \times 2 \times 5 \div (12 - 2) =$ _____

8. $6 + 12 \times 2 - 8 \div 2 + 2 \times 5 =$ _____

▲ Add or subtract.

1.
```
   639.253
 2,694.398
+    72.8123
```

2.
```
   73.21
−  25.24516
```

3.
```
   2.97
−  0.25346
```

4.
```
   352.977
 4,294.24
+   527.6477
```

▲ Use front-end estimation to estimate each sum or difference.

1.
```
   6,352
+  2,981
```

2.
```
 7,298,224
− 1,734,923
```

3.
```
   982,510
−  432,516
```

4.
```
 7,892,006
+ 3,674,997
```

5.
```
   416,739
+  317,473
```

6.
```
   7,299
−  3,176
```

Bonus Box: Change the parentheses from the order of operations problems to obtain the following different answers. Change number 1 to equal 57. Change number 5 to equal 128. Change number 8 to equal 26.

▲ Use the correct order of operations.

1. $(4 + 8) \div 4 + 4 \times 2 =$ _____

2. $16 - 10 \div 2 + 18 \div 3 + 3 =$ _____

3. $5 \times (18 - 9) - 6 \times (2 + 4) =$ _____

4. $(16 - 10) \div 2 - 10 \div (2 + 3) =$ _____

5. $(3 + 6) \times (10 - 6) \div 6 =$ _____

6. $3 \times 1 \div 3 + 2 \times (6 - 5) =$ _____

7. $20 \div 5 \times (10 - 3 \times 3) =$ _____

8. $(11 - 81 \div 9) \times (3 + 4) =$ _____

▲ Add or subtract.

1.
$$43.8792$$
$$+\ 628.3192$$

2.
$$152.76$$
$$-\ 143.6843$$

3.
$$5.708$$
$$-\ 2.8999$$

4.
$$526.178$$
$$+\ 265.9245$$

▲ Multiply or divide.

1. $6 \times 6 =$ _____

2. $5 \times 7 =$ _____

3. $49 \div 7 =$ _____

4. $64 \div 8 =$ _____

5. $9 \times 6 =$ _____

6. $7 \times 8 =$ _____

7. $24 \div 6 =$ _____

8. $7 \times 9 =$ _____

9. $21 \div 3 =$ _____

10. $27 \div 9 =$ _____

11. $4 \times 8 =$ _____

12. $8 \times 6 =$ _____

13. $54 \div 6 =$ _____

14. $42 \div 7 =$ _____

15. $36 \div 4 =$ _____

Bonus Box: Change the parentheses from the order of operations problems to obtain the following different answers. Change number 1 to equal 10. Change number 1 to equal 14. Change number 2 to equal 6.

Name _____

▲ On lined paper, arrange in columns and add. Write the sums here.

1. $4.56 + 21.35 + 3.5783 + 421.55 + 2.39784 =$ _____

2. $0.24 + 61.72908 + 31.526 + 6.733 + 2.19807 =$ _____

3. $1.62735 + 34.256 + 2.536 + 1.9807 + 32.546 =$ _____

4. $65.27 + 0.2537 + 4.1627 + 21.453 + 28.3256 =$ _____

5. $3.647 + 72.532 + 0.1253 + 6.85934 + 2.5373 =$ _____

6. $90.893 + 3.6 + 26.738 + 4.321 + 46.73 + 4.563 =$ _____

▲ Draw two pictures for each fraction. Illustrate the fraction as part of a whole and then as part of a group. The first one is done for you.

1. $\dfrac{4}{5}$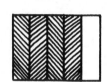

2. $\dfrac{1}{7}$

3. $\dfrac{3}{8}$

4. $\dfrac{2}{3}$

5. $\dfrac{8}{9}$

6. $\dfrac{5}{9}$

▲ Use the correct order of operations.

1. $12 \div 6 - 2 + 1 \times 8 + 6 =$ _____

2. $(16 - 8 \div 2) \times (3 + 4) - 10 =$ _____

3. $(10 - 2 \times 5) \times 16 \times 93 =$ _____

4. $(3 \times 3 - 4) \times 4 \div (2 - 1) =$ _____

Bonus Box: Change the parentheses from the order of operations problems to obtain the following different answers. Change number 1 to equal 17. Change number 2 to equal 6. Change number 4 to equal 15.

Name _____

▲ Subtract.

1. 23.145 – 0.0087 = _____

2. 7.835 – 6.0007 = _____

3. 152.6 – 26.3554 = _____

4. 16.3744 – 0.009 = _____

5. 54.6344 – 8.07 = _____

6. 45.263 – 2.75 = _____

▲ Multiply or divide the numerator and denominator by the same number to make an equivalent fraction. The first one is done for you.

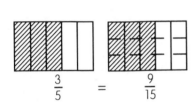

$$\frac{3}{5} = \frac{9}{15}$$

1. $\frac{3}{5} \times \frac{3}{3} = \frac{9}{15}$

2. $\frac{6}{12} \div \frac{2}{2} = \frac{3}{\_}$

3. $\frac{4}{10} \div \frac{\_}{\_} = \frac{\_}{5}$

4. $\frac{1}{3} \times \frac{\_}{\_} = \frac{4}{\_}$

5. $\frac{2}{6} \times \frac{\_}{\_} = \frac{\_}{12}$

6. $\frac{7}{8} \times \frac{\_}{\_} = \frac{14}{\_}$

7. $\frac{10}{12} \div \frac{\_}{\_} = \frac{5}{\_}$

8. $\frac{3}{4} \times \frac{\_}{\_} = \frac{\_}{8}$

▲ Find the area of each figure.

1. 8 m, 8 m _____ m²

2. 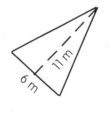 11 m, 6 m _____ m²

3. 27 m, 44 m _____ m²

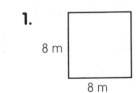

Bonus Box: Choose six fractions from above. For each fraction, write two other equivalent fractions.

© Carson-Dellosa   IF87123 • Mixed Skills in Math 5-6

Name _____

▲ Add or subtract.

1. 5.6 + 3.253 + 12.008 + 35.26 + 0.092001 + 3.3 = _____

2. 12.460 – 12.362709 = _____

3. 2.00705 – 0.0235167 = _____

4. 3.456 + 21.5377 + 0.035 + 46.3522 + 0.008 = _____

▲ Complete the equivalent fractions.

1.
$$\frac{2}{6} = \frac{}{3}$$

2.
$$\frac{5}{20} = \frac{1}{}$$

3.
$$\frac{6}{7} = \frac{}{14}$$

4.
$$\frac{2}{7} = \frac{}{28}$$

5.
$$\frac{6}{8} = \frac{36}{}$$

6.
$$\frac{5}{9} = \frac{}{63}$$

7.
$$\frac{21}{49} = \frac{3}{}$$

8.
$$\frac{1}{3} = \frac{}{24}$$

9.
$$\frac{4}{5} = \frac{28}{}$$

10.
$$\frac{2}{3} = \frac{}{15}$$

11.
$$\frac{12}{16} = \frac{}{4}$$

12.
$$\frac{4}{6} = \frac{16}{}$$

▲ Write the value of the underlined digit. The first one is done for you.

1.   574,3<u>8</u>9,002

   eighty thousand

2.   92<u>3</u>,510,367

   _____

3.   251,627,<u>8</u>33

   _____

4.   72,<u>8</u>93,271

   _____

5.   4,29<u>8</u>,781,254

   _____

6.   5<u>6</u>3,334,908

   _____

Bonus Box: Write the above six number words in order from least to greatest.

Name _____

▲ Add or subtract.

1. 7.45 + 82.1209 + 3.264 + 33.23348 + 6.35 = _____

2. 4.608 – 2.463754 = _____

3. 2.425 – 0.0087653 = _____

4. 55.2537 + 2.51667 + 0.112113 + 46.3 + 4.4 = _____

▲ Simplify each fraction to lowest terms. The first one is done for you.

1.
$$\frac{3}{12} = \frac{1}{4}$$

2.
$$\frac{12}{18} = \underline{\quad}$$

3.
$$\frac{32}{40} = \underline{\quad}$$

4.
$$\frac{27}{33} = \underline{\quad}$$

5.
$$\frac{48}{56} = \underline{\quad}$$

6.
$$\frac{7}{21} = \underline{\quad}$$

7.
$$\frac{36}{63} = \underline{\quad}$$

8.
$$\frac{56}{63} = \underline{\quad}$$

9.
$$\frac{8}{20} = \underline{\quad}$$

10.
$$\frac{42}{48} = \underline{\quad}$$

11.
$$\frac{21}{28} = \underline{\quad}$$

12.
$$\frac{35}{49} = \underline{\quad}$$

▲ Write the value of the underlined digit. The first one is done for you.

1. 7,894,343,263
   eight hundred million

2. 426,893
   _____

3. 9,219,807,235
   _____

4. 23,516,738,543
   _____

5. 355,638,234
   _____

6. 947,382,376
   _____

Bonus Box: Choose four numbers from above. Write them in expanded form.

Name _____

▲ Multiply.

1.	2.	3.	4.	5.
246 x 7	268 x 9	432 x 6	314 x 2	621 x 5

6.	7.	8.	9.	10.
853 x 3	743 x 8	830 x 4	946 x 5	362 x 7

▲ Simplify each fraction to lowest terms.

▲ Record the perimeter of each figure.

1.
$$\frac{25}{45} = \underline{\quad}$$

2.
$$\frac{18}{21} = \underline{\quad}$$

3.
$$\frac{6}{48} = \underline{\quad}$$

4.
$$\frac{14}{63} = \underline{\quad}$$

5.
$$\frac{46}{92} = \underline{\quad}$$

6.
$$\frac{12}{20} = \underline{\quad}$$

7.
$$\frac{8}{10} = \underline{\quad}$$

8.
$$\frac{36}{40} = \underline{\quad}$$

9.
$$\frac{9}{12} = \underline{\quad}$$

10.
$$\frac{12}{21} = \underline{\quad}$$

11.
$$\frac{4}{12} = \underline{\quad}$$

12.
$$\frac{36}{42} = \underline{\quad}$$

1.

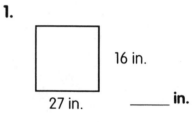

16 in.

27 in. _____ **in.**

2.

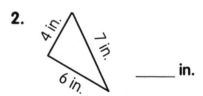

4 in. 7 in. 6 in.

_____ **in.**

3.

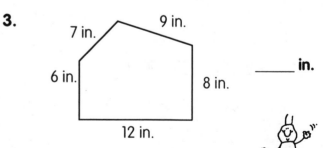

9 in.
7 in.
6 in. 8 in.
12 in.

_____ **in.**

Bonus Box: Write five numbers with fewer than ten digits so that the digits in each number have a sum of 40.

Name _____

▲ Multiply.

1. 352
x 4

2. 673
x 2

3. 708
x 9

4. 256
x 6

5. 824
x 3

6. 518
x 5

7. 472
x 6

8. 269
x 8

9. 486
x 7

10. 675
x 5

▲ Rename each fraction as a mixed or whole number. The first one is done for you.

1. $\dfrac{7}{3}$ = $2\dfrac{1}{3}$

2. $\dfrac{24}{5}$ = ___

3. $\dfrac{15}{2}$ = ___

4. $\dfrac{24}{4}$ = ___

5. $\dfrac{35}{4}$ = ___

6. $\dfrac{23}{7}$ = ___

7. $\dfrac{50}{9}$ = ___

8. $\dfrac{17}{6}$ = ___

▲ On lined paper, arrange in columns and add. Record the sums here.

1. 5,637 + 89 + 243 + 891 + 4,553 + 74 + 372 = _____

2. 902 + 654 + 3,995 + 45 + 721 +88 + 39 + 536 = _____

3. 68 + 432 + 1,894 + 79 + 245 + 426 +7,350 = _____

Bonus Box: Write six numbers that when rounded to the nearest tenth, round to 243.8. Include numbers that round up and numbers that round down.

▲ Multiply.

1.
536
x 27

2.
604
x 18

3.
451
x 41

4.
846
x 39

5.
524
x 26

6.
627
x 53

7.
892
x 34

8.
931
x 29

▲ Rename each fraction as a mixed or whole number.

1. $\dfrac{17}{4}$ = ___

2. $\dfrac{16}{2}$ = ___

3. $\dfrac{46}{5}$ = ___

4. $\dfrac{23}{6}$ = ___

5. $\dfrac{18}{7}$ = ___

6. $\dfrac{17}{3}$ = ___

7. $\dfrac{17}{9}$ = ___

8. $\dfrac{12}{3}$ = ___

▲ Add.

1.
35.2635
3,256.229
+ 399.5896

2.
3.25617
35.72897
+ 0.892313

3.
5.4737
7.278354
+ 82.46735

4.
76.37
0.68362
+ 61.3785

Bonus Box: Write five fractions equivalent to $\dfrac{2}{3}$.

▲ Multiply.

1.
427
x 57

2.
836
x 49

3.
632
x 66

4.
518
x 27

5.
942
x 15

6.
643
x 74

7.
782
x 81

8.
385
x 42

9.
468
x 65

10.
563
x 73

▲ Rename each as an improper fraction.

1.
$2\frac{3}{5}$ = ——

2.
$4\frac{7}{8}$ = ——

3.
$6\frac{1}{2}$ = ——

4.
$8\frac{2}{3}$ = ——

5.
$5\frac{3}{4}$ = ——

6.
$7\frac{1}{3}$ = ——

7.
$3\frac{5}{6}$ = ——

8.
$4\frac{1}{4}$ = ——

▲ Add or subtract.

1. $6.77 + 2.0093 + 42.553 + 3.64708 + 0.002435 =$ _____

2. $5.621 - 2.78390233 =$ _____

3. $0.9278 + 4.36277 + 3.462 + 6.37453 + 6.63 =$ _____

4. $72.34 - 66.284315 =$ _____

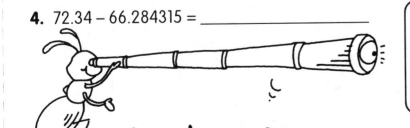

Bonus Box: Eight coins are in a bank. Exactly three-fourths are pennies. What could be the value of the coins in the bank? Provide two possibilities.

Name _____

▲ Multiply.

1.
```
  924
x  33
```

2.
```
  426
x  46
```

3.
```
  623
x  52
```

4.
```
  552
x  37
```

5.
```
  826
x  12
```

6.
```
  638
x  69
```

7.
```
  314
x  87
```

8.
```
  147
x  68
```

9.
```
  475
x  83
```

▲ Rename each as an improper fraction.

1. $5\frac{4}{7} = $ —

2. $1\frac{4}{9} = $ —

3. $2\frac{3}{4} = $ —

4. $8\frac{2}{3} = $ —

5. $6\frac{1}{4} = $ —

6. $9\frac{1}{2} = $ —

7. $3\frac{4}{5} = $ —

8. $2\frac{5}{8} = $ —

▲ Add or subtract.

1.
```
   4.36
   2.678
+ 46.8379
```

2.
```
   4.567
- 3.647833
```

3.
```
   3.2876
  25.873
+ 38.92083
```

4.
```
  46.89
   0.52617
+ 78.9263
```

Bonus Box: Write five 7-digit numbers that are even. The sum of the digits in each number is 29.

▲ Divide.

1.
$6\overline{)2,736}$

2.
$8\overline{)5,144}$

3.
$2\overline{)1,834}$

4.
$7\overline{)3,983}$

5.
$5\overline{)3,540}$

6.
$9\overline{)4,239}$

▲ Add the fractions.

1.
$\dfrac{1}{5} + \dfrac{3}{5} = $ ___

2.
$\dfrac{4}{6} + \dfrac{1}{6} = $ ___

3.
$\dfrac{1}{3} + \dfrac{1}{3} = $ ___

4.
$\dfrac{5}{8} + \dfrac{2}{8} = $ ___

▲ Simplify each fraction to lowest terms.

1.
$\dfrac{12}{8} = $ ___

2.
$\dfrac{15}{27} = $ ___

3.
$\dfrac{42}{48} = $ ___

4.
$\dfrac{28}{35} = $ ___

5.
$\dfrac{18}{63} = $ ___

6.
$\dfrac{23}{46} = $ ___

7.
$\dfrac{48}{88} = $ ___

8.
$\dfrac{18}{24} = $ ___

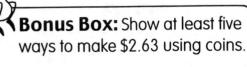

Bonus Box: Show at least five ways to make $2.63 using coins.

Name _____

▲ Divide.

1.
$$5\overline{)3{,}717}$$

2.
$$9\overline{)3{,}678}$$

3.
$$4\overline{)2{,}536}$$

4.
$$8\overline{)2{,}181}$$

5.
$$3\overline{)2{,}614}$$

6.
$$6\overline{)1{,}186}$$

7.
$$7\overline{)2{,}564}$$

8.
$$9\overline{)5{,}162}$$

▲ Add the fractions. Simplify each sum to lowest terms. The first one is done for you.

1. $\dfrac{1}{6} + \dfrac{2}{6} = \dfrac{2}{6} = \dfrac{1}{2}$

2. $\dfrac{3}{10} + \dfrac{5}{10} = \underline{} = \underline{}$

3. $\dfrac{4}{9} + \dfrac{2}{9} = \underline{} = \underline{}$

4. $\dfrac{5}{12} + \dfrac{5}{12} = \underline{} = \underline{}$

5. $\dfrac{1}{4} + \dfrac{1}{4} = \underline{} = \underline{}$

6. $\dfrac{3}{16} + \dfrac{5}{16} = \underline{} = \underline{}$

▲ Write the greatest common factor of each set of numbers.

1. 140 and 120 _____

2. 84 and 231 _____

3. 315 and 60 _____

4. 40 and 168 _____

5. 270 and 180 _____

6. 168 and 189 _____

Bonus Box: Sketch five different rectangles. Assign each side a length and give the area for each figure.

Name _____

▲ Divide.

1.
46 | 16,192

2.
27 | 18,468

3.
59 | 25,429

4.
83 | 61,918

5.
78 | 48,438

6.
65 | 53,040

▲ Add the fractions. Reduce each sum to simplest terms. The first one is done for you.

1.
$\frac{5}{14} + \frac{3}{14} = \frac{8}{14} = \frac{4}{7}$

2.
$\frac{1}{6} + \frac{3}{6} = \underline{} = \underline{}$

3.
$\frac{7}{18} + \frac{2}{18} = \underline{} = \underline{}$

4.
$\frac{4}{10} + \frac{1}{10} = \underline{} = \underline{}$

5.
$\frac{1}{8} + \frac{1}{8} = \underline{} = \underline{}$

6.
$\frac{5}{24} + \frac{3}{24} = \underline{} = \underline{}$

▲ Use the chart to answer the questions.

Fifth Graders in Clubs				
Club Name	Drama	Chess	Spanish	Technology
# of Students	36	21	48	63

• Which club has 21 members? _____

• How many fifth graders are in the drama club? _____

• What is the total club membership? _____

• Which club has the greatest number of members?

_____

Bonus Box: Use the information in the chart to make a pictograph. Make a key with a symbol that stands for three students.

▲ Divide.

1. 21 ⟌ 13,272

2. 49 ⟌ 23,569

3. 73 ⟌ 23,579

4. 74 ⟌ 26,566

5. 85 ⟌ 60,605

6. 16 ⟌ 2,368

▲ Add the fractions. Simplify each sum to lowest terms.

1. $\dfrac{3}{12} + \dfrac{6}{12}$ = —— = ——

2. $\dfrac{3}{6} + \dfrac{1}{6}$ = —— = ——

3. $\dfrac{13}{18} + \dfrac{2}{18}$ = —— = ——

4. $\dfrac{7}{10} + \dfrac{1}{10}$ = —— = ——

5. $\dfrac{5}{14} + \dfrac{3}{14}$ = —— = ——

6. $\dfrac{1}{8} + \dfrac{5}{8}$ = —— = ——

▲ Refer to the chart to answer the questions.

Movies Watched by Fifth- and Sixth-Grade Students				
Week	Comedy	Horror	Romance	Action
1	72	56	24	66
2	48	72	13	84
3	65	90	31	74
4	52	89	35	97

• What is the total number of movies watched in week three? _____

• How many horror movies were watched during the four weeks? _____

• In which week were the fewest movies watched? _____

• Which type of movie was watched the most? _____

Bonus Box: The school purchases two bottles of glue for every 5 people. How many bottles of glue are purchased if there are 45 students? 150 students? 260 students?

Name _____

▲ Divide.

1.
$$94 \overline{)40{,}984}$$

2.
$$27 \overline{)19{,}170}$$

3.
$$46 \overline{)5{,}934}$$

4.
$$19 \overline{)17{,}898}$$

5.
$$38 \overline{)21{,}508}$$

6.
$$83 \overline{)22{,}659}$$

▲ Add the fractions. Simplify each sum to lowest terms.

1. $\dfrac{3}{16} + \dfrac{5}{16} + \dfrac{2}{16} = \underline{} = \underline{}$

2. $\dfrac{2}{15} + \dfrac{7}{15} + \dfrac{1}{15} = \underline{} = \underline{}$

3. $\dfrac{1}{8} + \dfrac{2}{8} + \dfrac{3}{8} = \underline{} = \underline{}$

4. $\dfrac{4}{10} + \dfrac{1}{10} + \dfrac{3}{10} = \underline{} = \underline{}$

5. $\dfrac{6}{20} + \dfrac{5}{20} + \dfrac{1}{20} = \underline{} = \underline{}$

6. $\dfrac{2}{9} + \dfrac{1}{9} + \dfrac{3}{9} = \underline{} = \underline{}$

▲ Refer to the chart to answer the questions.

Plant Height in Inches				
Plant	Week 1	Week 2	Week 3	Week 4
A	0	$\dfrac{1}{4}$	$1\dfrac{1}{16}$	$4\dfrac{3}{4}$
B	$\dfrac{1}{16}$	$\dfrac{1}{2}$	1	$5\dfrac{3}{16}$

• How much did plant A grow each week?

Week 1 _____ Week 2 _____ Week 3 _____

Week 4 _____

• How much did plant B grow each week?

Week 1 _____ Week 2 _____ Week 3 _____

Week 4 _____

Bonus Box: Draw the actual heights of the two plants each of the four weeks. Organize and label your drawings.

Name _____

▲ Divide.

1.
39) 9,610

2.
97) 54,575

3.
41) 28,416

4.
69) 55,498

5.
84) 61,395

6.
52) 44,880

▲ Subtract the fractions. Simplify to lowest terms. The first one is done for you.

1.
$$\frac{11}{12} - \frac{5}{12} = \frac{6}{12} = \frac{1}{2}$$

2.
$$\frac{4}{9} - \frac{1}{9} = — = —$$

3.
$$\frac{7}{16} - \frac{1}{16} = — = —$$

4.
$$\frac{9}{10} - \frac{3}{10} = — = —$$

5.
$$\frac{19}{21} - \frac{5}{21} = — = —$$

6.
$$\frac{4}{6} - \frac{1}{6} = — = —$$

▲ Record the volume of each figure.

1.
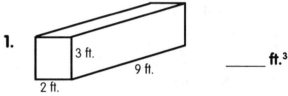
3 ft.
9 ft.
2 ft.
_____ ft.³

2.
20 mm
46 mm
32 mm
_____ mm³

3.
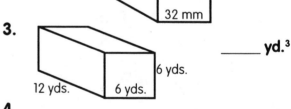
6 yds.
12 yds.
6 yds.
_____ yd.³

4.
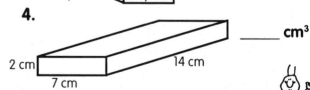
2 cm
14 cm
7 cm
_____ cm³

Bonus Box: The swimming pool provides 3 towels for every 7 students. How many towels do they need if there are 56 students? 133 students? 259 students?

54

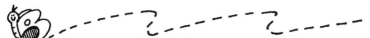

▲ Divide.

1.
$$61 \overline{)56{,}486}$$

2.
$$48 \overline{)27{,}421}$$

3.
$$16 \overline{)7{,}720}$$

4.
$$79 \overline{)27{,}270}$$

5.
$$39 \overline{)23{,}908}$$

6.
$$60 \overline{)29{,}300}$$

▲ Subtract the fractions. Simplify to lowest terms.

1.
$$\frac{5}{8} - \frac{3}{8} = \underline{\quad} = \underline{\quad}$$

2.
$$\frac{7}{12} - \frac{1}{12} = \underline{\quad} = \underline{\quad}$$

3.
$$\frac{3}{4} - \frac{1}{4} = \underline{\quad} = \underline{\quad}$$

4.
$$\frac{17}{20} - \frac{5}{20} = \underline{\quad} = \underline{\quad}$$

5.
$$\frac{11}{14} - \frac{3}{14} = \underline{\quad} = \underline{\quad}$$

6.
$$\frac{8}{9} - \frac{2}{9} = \underline{\quad} = \underline{\quad}$$

▲ Record the volume of each figure.

1.

13 m
23 m
6 m
_____ **m³**

2.

2 m
4 m
12 m
_____ **m³**

3.

16 cm
16 cm
16 cm
_____ **cm³**

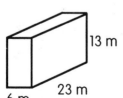

Bonus Box: Six coins are in a bank. Exactly one-third are dimes. What could be the value of the coins in the bank? Provide two possibilities.

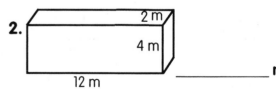

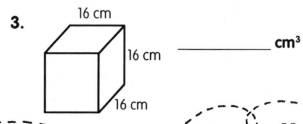

Name _____

▲ Multiply or divide.

1.
$$697 \times 68$$

2.
$$86 \overline{)50{,}830}$$

3.
$$28 \overline{)13{,}216}$$

4.
$$364 \times 73$$

5.
$$64 \overline{)57{,}156}$$

6.
$$71 \overline{)24{,}995}$$

▲ Subtract the fractions. Simplify to lowest terms.

1.
$$2\frac{3}{4} - 1\frac{1}{4}$$

2.
$$5\frac{5}{6} - 2\frac{1}{6}$$

3.
$$7\frac{7}{10} - 5\frac{2}{10}$$

4.
$$3\frac{6}{7} - 1\frac{5}{7}$$

5.
$$4\frac{13}{14} - 1\frac{3}{14}$$

6.
$$8\frac{2}{3} - 4\frac{1}{3}$$

▲ Record the volume of each figure.

1.
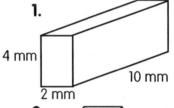
4 mm   10 mm   2 mm

_____ mm³

2.
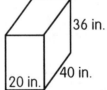
36 in.   40 in.   20 in.

_____ in.³

3.
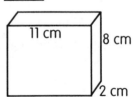
11 cm   8 cm   2 cm

_____ cm³

Bonus Box: Write six numbers that when rounded to the nearest hundredth, round to 354.29. Include numbers that round up and numbers that round down.

© Carson-Dellosa   IF87123 • Mixed Skills in Math 5-6

▲ Multiply or divide.

1.
$$\begin{array}{r} 241 \\ \times\ 96 \\ \hline \end{array}$$

2.
$$73\overline{)37{,}100}$$

3.
$$62\overline{)14{,}635}$$

4.
$$\begin{array}{r} 355 \\ \times\ 88 \\ \hline \end{array}$$

5.
$$39\overline{)22{,}485}$$

6.
$$46\overline{)43{,}342}$$

▲ Add or subtract the fractions. Simplify each answer to lowest terms.

1.
$$\begin{array}{r} 5\frac{7}{9} \\ -\ 2\frac{4}{9} \\ \hline \end{array}$$

2.
$$\begin{array}{r} 2\frac{1}{6} \\ +\ 5\frac{2}{6} \\ \hline \end{array}$$

3.
$$\begin{array}{r} 4\frac{5}{10} \\ +\ 3\frac{3}{10} \\ \hline \end{array}$$

4.
$$\begin{array}{r} 9\frac{7}{12} \\ -\ 3\frac{3}{12} \\ \hline \end{array}$$

5.
$$\begin{array}{r} 2\frac{5}{14} \\ +\ 4\frac{3}{14} \\ \hline \end{array}$$

6.
$$\begin{array}{r} 9\frac{3}{4} \\ -\ 5\frac{1}{4} \\ \hline \end{array}$$

▲ Use the correct order of operations.

1. $4 \times (2 - 2) + 8 \div 4 =$ _____

2. $(2 + 5 - 1) \times 6 - 10 \div 2 =$ _____

3. $(8 - 6 \div 2) \times (12 \div 2 - 4) =$ _____

4. $18 - 5 \times 2 + 3 \times 6 \div 2 =$ _____

5. $(2 + 6) \div 4 \times 2 + 10 =$ _____

6. $6 \times 5 \div 10 - 8 \div (2 + 2) =$ _____

Bonus Box: Change the parentheses from the order of operations problems to obtain the following different answers. Change number 3 to equal 6. Change number 4 to equal 35.

Name _____

▲ Multiply.

1.
$$\begin{array}{r} 23.1 \\ \times\ 4.6 \\ \hline \end{array}$$

2.
$$\begin{array}{r} 6.19 \\ \times\ .05 \\ \hline \end{array}$$

3.
$$\begin{array}{r} 8.06 \\ \times\ 74 \\ \hline \end{array}$$

4.
$$\begin{array}{r} .097 \\ \times\ .88 \\ \hline \end{array}$$

5.
$$\begin{array}{r} 9.35 \\ \times\ .37 \\ \hline \end{array}$$

6.
$$\begin{array}{r} 8.94 \\ \times\ .06 \\ \hline \end{array}$$

7.
$$\begin{array}{r} .048 \\ \times\ 8.3 \\ \hline \end{array}$$

8.
$$\begin{array}{r} 371 \\ \times\ .32 \\ \hline \end{array}$$

▲ Add the fractions. Write each answer as a mixed numeral. Simplify to lowest terms. The first one is done for you.

1.
$$\frac{7}{9} + \frac{4}{9} = 1\frac{1}{2}$$

2.
$$\frac{2}{3} + \frac{2}{3} =$$

3.
$$\frac{9}{10} + \frac{7}{10} =$$

4.
$$\frac{1}{2} + \frac{5}{2} =$$

5.
$$\frac{7}{3} + \frac{2}{3} =$$

6.
$$\frac{5}{6} + \frac{4}{6} =$$

▲ Refer to the chart to answer the questions.

• How many students were polled? _____

• Which type of location had the most students?

  _____

• How many more students stayed home than

  went skiing? _____

• What fraction of students went to an amusement park? Give your answer in simplest terms.

  _____

Spring Vacation Destinations

Type of Location	# of Students
home	68
beach	79
amusement park	58
skiing	46
other	39

Bonus Box: Show at least five ways to make $3.46 using coins.

▲ Multiply.

1.	2.	3.	4.	5.
7.62 x .09	.642 x 67	59.1 x .22	.005 x .04	6.75 x .98

6.	7.	8.	9.	10.
6.87 x 5.1	6.02 x 6.8	217 x 6.9	4.77 x .04	1.06 x 2.3

▲ Add the fractions. Simplify to lowest terms.

1.
$$2\frac{1}{2} + 5\frac{3}{2}$$

2.
$$4\frac{6}{15} + 1\frac{4}{15}$$

3.
$$1\frac{9}{10} + 2\frac{9}{10}$$

4.
$$5\frac{2}{3} + 6\frac{1}{3}$$

5.
$$3\frac{7}{8} + 7\frac{5}{8}$$

6.
$$3\frac{4}{5} + 5\frac{3}{5}$$

▲ Write the numeral for each number word.

1. One hundred forty-five billion, sixty-seven

_____

2. Two hundred fifty-one thousandths

_____

3. Six hundred seven billion, sixty-four million, six hundred thirteen and thirty-two ten-thousandths

_____

4. Fourteen and five hundred eight thousandths

_____

Bonus Box: Write five numbers with seven digits each. The digits in each number have a sum of 39.

Name _____

▲ Multiply.

1. 567 x 3.4	2. 1.44 x .05	3. 4.62 x 76	4. .072 x .24	5. 79.8 x 6.3

6. .473 x 79	7. 7.52 x .07	8. 34.6 x 2.7	9. 832 x .18	10. .004 x 6.2

▲ Add the fractions. Simplify to lowest terms.

1.
$$4 \frac{4}{7}$$
$$+ 1 \frac{6}{7}$$

2.
$$\frac{10}{3}$$
$$+ 4 \frac{8}{3}$$

3.
$$5 \frac{3}{10}$$
$$+ 2 \frac{9}{10}$$

4.
$$7 \frac{13}{21}$$
$$+ 1 \frac{15}{21}$$

5.
$$2 \frac{3}{2}$$
$$+ 4 \frac{1}{2}$$

6.
$$1 \frac{17}{20}$$
$$+ 7 \frac{13}{20}$$

▲ Add or subtract.

1. $4.573 + 2.0064 + 0.005 + 2.4109 + 5.16 + 0.06 =$ _____

2. $42.61 - 8.352401 =$ _____

3. $0.3628 - 0.3619346 =$ _____

4. $6.27 + 0.462 + 0.0084 + 3.362 + 53.5005 =$

_____

Bonus Box: Write the products from the multiplication problems in order from least to greatest.

▲ Divide.

1.
$$.4 \overline{\smash{)}14.6}$$

2.
$$.07 \overline{\smash{)}1.729}$$

3.
$$6 \overline{\smash{)}47.34}$$

4.
$$.9 \overline{\smash{)}0.4347}$$

5.
$$.2 \overline{\smash{)}1.152}$$

6.
$$3 \overline{\smash{)}179.4}$$

7.
$$.004 \overline{\smash{)}.3252}$$

8.
$$.05 \overline{\smash{)}.337}$$

▲ Add the fractions. Simplify to lowest terms.

1.
$$2 \frac{7}{8}$$
$$+ 3 \frac{5}{8}$$

2.
$$4 \frac{2}{3}$$
$$+ 1 \frac{2}{3}$$

3.
$$3 \frac{8}{12}$$
$$+ 2 \frac{7}{12}$$

4.
$$1 \frac{5}{6}$$
$$+ 2 \frac{5}{6}$$

5.
$$2 \frac{3}{10}$$
$$+ 5 \frac{7}{10}$$

6.
$$3 \frac{13}{16}$$
$$+ 1 \frac{15}{16}$$

▲ Find the volume of each figure.

1.

10 m
10 m
90 m
_____ **m³**

2.

28 cm
8 cm
11 cm
_____ **cm³**

3.

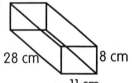

3 in.
5 in.
7 in.
_____ **in.³**

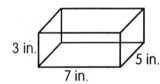

Bonus Box: The cafeteria plans to provide seven apples for every 12 students. How many apples will they provide for 72 people? 108 people? 144 people?

Name _____

▲ Divide.

1. .09 | .5049

2. .6 | 43.74

3. .04 | .2936

4. 8 | 674.4

5. .7 | .1057

6. .003 | 2.382

7. .08 | 2.6

8. .3 | 279.9

▲ Subtract the fractions. Simplify to lowest terms.

1.
$$4 \frac{4}{7}$$
$$- 2 \frac{6}{7}$$

2.
$$5 \frac{1}{3}$$
$$- 1 \frac{2}{3}$$

3.
$$7 \frac{4}{10}$$
$$- 2 \frac{9}{10}$$

4.
$$3 \frac{3}{8}$$
$$- 1 \frac{7}{8}$$

▲ Add or subtract.

1.
   68.35
   59.005
+ 893.266

2.
   1,574.8
− 539.936

3.
      0.006
   2,789.361
+ 5,836.89

4.
   3.7004
   0.893
+ 45.8049

5.
   156.2
− 156.179

6.
   5.9001
− 4.89362

Bonus Box: Write five fractions equivalent to $\frac{3}{4}$.

Name _____

▲ Divide.

1.
$$.23\overline{)1.7227}$$

2.
$$1.2\overline{)44.88}$$

3.
$$36\overline{)1,054.8}$$

4.
$$.007\overline{)4.718}$$

5.
$$.043\overline{).04515}$$

6.
$$5.8\overline{)138.04}$$

Bonus Box: Eight coins are in a bank. Exactly one-fourth are nickels, and exactly one-half are dimes. What could be the value of the coins in the bank? Provide two possibilities.

▲ Subtract the fractions. Simplify to lowest terms.

1.
$$3\frac{2}{5}$$
$$-1\frac{4}{5}$$

2.
$$4\frac{1}{4}$$
$$-2\frac{3}{4}$$

3.
$$6\frac{5}{9}$$
$$-1\frac{8}{9}$$

4.
$$5\frac{7}{16}$$
$$-2\frac{9}{16}$$

▲ Sketch each fraction. Then order each set of fractions from least to greatest.

1.
$$\frac{1}{2} \qquad \frac{3}{4} \qquad \frac{2}{5}$$

_____

2.
$$\frac{2}{3} \qquad \frac{3}{4} \qquad \frac{5}{6}$$

_____

3.
$$\frac{1}{4} \qquad \frac{1}{2} \qquad \frac{5}{8}$$

_____

4.
$$\frac{5}{7} \qquad \frac{1}{3} \qquad \frac{6}{21}$$

_____

Name _____

▲ Divide.

1.

$.053\overline{)1.2031}$

2.

$31\overline{)15.128}$

3.

$5.9\overline{)32.332}$

4.

$.03\overline{)21.54}$

5.

$.62\overline{)2.7962}$

6.

$.0048\overline{).6624}$

Bonus Box: Find and trace 12 angles. Label each right angle, acute angle, or obtuse angle.

▲ Subtract the fractions. Simplify to lowest terms.

1.

$5\dfrac{7}{10}$
$-2\dfrac{9}{10}$

2.

$3\dfrac{1}{2}$
$-1\dfrac{2}{2}$

3.

$4\dfrac{1}{4}$
$-3\dfrac{2}{4}$

4.

$8\dfrac{7}{14}$
$-3\dfrac{9}{14}$

▲ Sketch each fraction. Then order each set of fractions from least to greatest.

1.

$\dfrac{6}{8}$ $\dfrac{1}{2}$ $\dfrac{3}{4}$

_____

2.

$\dfrac{1}{5}$ $\dfrac{2}{3}$ $\dfrac{3}{5}$

_____

3.

$\dfrac{5}{6}$ $\dfrac{2}{3}$ $\dfrac{1}{2}$

_____

4.

$\dfrac{4}{9}$ $\dfrac{2}{3}$ $\dfrac{5}{6}$

_____

Name _____

▲ Divide.

1.

$6.2\overline{)12.586}$

2.

$.0091\overline{).48048}$

3.

$.29\overline{).9628}$

4.

$.037\overline{).005698}$

5.

$58\overline{)46.168}$

6.

$8.3\overline{)549.46}$

Bonus Box: The store is selling 3 cookies for 61¢. How much will it cost for 21 cookies? How many cookies can you get for $2.44?

▲ Subtract the fractions. Simplify to lowest terms.

1.

$4\frac{2}{5}$
$-1\frac{4}{5}$
$\overline{}$

2.

$7\frac{3}{14}$
$-2\frac{7}{14}$
$\overline{}$

3.

$6\frac{2}{10}$
$-4\frac{8}{10}$
$\overline{}$

4.

$8\frac{2}{6}$
$-2\frac{5}{6}$
$\overline{}$

▲ Write each decimal. Change each decimal to a percent.

	Decimal	Percent
1. sixteen hundredths	_____	_____
2. eighty-nine hundredths	_____	_____
3. fifty-three hundredths	_____	_____
4. nine hundredths	_____	_____
5. seventy-one hundredths	_____	_____
6. twenty-seven hundredths	_____	_____

Name _____

▲ Multiply or divide.

1.
$$24.1 \times 7.2$$

2.
$$4.1\overline{)152.11}$$

3.
$$.039\overline{)18.057}$$

4.
$$.352 \times 6.3$$

5.
$$.0047\overline{).011656}$$

Bonus Box: Use grid paper to sketch five different shapes with an area of 16. Find the perimeter for each.

▲ Subtract the fractions. Simplify to lowest terms.

1.
$$3\frac{1}{2}$$
$$-2\frac{1}{2}$$

2.
$$6\frac{3}{4}$$
$$-2\frac{2}{4}$$

3.
$$4\frac{2}{9}$$
$$-1\frac{5}{9}$$

4.
$$3\frac{3}{16}$$
$$-1\frac{7}{16}$$

▲ Write each decimal. Change each decimal to a percent.

	Decimal	Percent
1. forty-five hundredths	_____	_____
2. eleven hundredths	_____	_____
3. eight hundredths	_____	_____
4. seventy-two hundredths	_____	_____
5. twenty-nine hundredths	_____	_____
6. fourteen hundredths	_____	_____

Name _____

▲ Multiply or divide.

1.
```
    4.09
  ×  .09
```

2.
```
69 ⟌ 359.49
```

3.
```
.74 ⟌ 5.957
```

4.
```
   .0056
 ×  7.8
```

5.
```
.24 ⟌ 1.5624
```

Bonus Box: Draw models for two of the fractions from the bottom of the page.

▲ Add or subtract the fractions. Simplify to lowest terms.

1.
$$6\frac{4}{21}$$
$$-2\frac{18}{21}$$

2.
$$6\frac{3}{16}$$
$$-4\frac{11}{16}$$

3.
$$4\frac{3}{7}$$
$$+1\frac{6}{7}$$

4.
$$3\frac{7}{9}$$
$$+2\frac{5}{9}$$

▲ Write each decimal. Change each decimal to a percent. Change the percents to fractions. Write the fractions in lowest terms.

	Decimal	Percent	Fraction
1. sixty hundredths	_____	_____	_____
2. thirty-eight hundredths	_____	_____	_____
3. fifteen hundredths	_____	_____	_____
4. ninety hundredths	_____	_____	_____
5. fifty-nine hundredths	_____	_____	_____
6. twenty-one hundredths	_____	_____	_____

Name _____

▲ Multiply or divide.

1.
$$36.8$$
$$\times \ \ 27$$

2.
$$4.2\overline{)39.858}$$

3.
$$.067\overline{).39865}$$

4.
$$5.66$$
$$\times \ .03$$

5.
$$.068\overline{).64736}$$

Bonus Box: Write five numbers that have eight digits each. The sum of the digits for each number is 42. The first digit is double the last digit.

▲ Find common denominators. Add the fractions. Simplify to lowest terms. The first one is done for you.

1.
$$\frac{1}{4} + \frac{1}{2} = \frac{1}{4} + \frac{2}{4} = \frac{3}{4}$$

2.
$$\frac{3}{5} + \frac{2}{3} =$$

3.
$$\frac{5}{8} + \frac{1}{4} =$$

4.
$$\frac{3}{10} + \frac{1}{5} =$$

▲ Write each decimal. Change each decimal to a percent. Change the percents to fractions. Write the fractions in lowest terms.

	Decimal	Percent	Fraction
1. thirty-nine hundredths	_____	_____	_____
2. two hundredths	_____	_____	_____
3. fifty-one hundredths	_____	_____	_____
4. eighty hundredths	_____	_____	_____
5. twelve hundredths	_____	_____	_____
6. eighty-three hundredths	_____	_____	_____

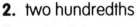

Name _____

▲ Find common denominators. Add the fractions. Simplify to lowest terms.

1.
$$\frac{2}{3} + \frac{1}{9} =$$

2.
$$\frac{2}{7} + \frac{1}{2} =$$

3.
$$\frac{4}{9} + \frac{1}{6} =$$

4.
$$\frac{1}{6} + \frac{1}{5} =$$

5.
$$\frac{2}{4} + \frac{1}{6} =$$

6.
$$\frac{2}{8} + \frac{1}{7} =$$

▲ Find the average of each set of numbers.

1. 456   273   802   321

_____

2. 5,803   240   4,637   3,672

_____

3. 649   317   253   761

_____

4. 56   21   79   49   43   28

_____

5. 21,114   11,314   41,117

_____

6. 99   163   266   290   87

_____

▲ Write each decimal. Change each decimal to a percent. Change the percents to fractions. Write the fractions in lowest terms.

	Decimal	Percent	Fraction
1. twenty-five hundredths	_____	_____	_____
2. six hundredths	_____	_____	_____
3. seventy-two hundredths	_____	_____	_____
4. twelve hundredths	_____	_____	_____

Bonus Box: You can buy 6 carnival tickets for 75¢. How many tickets can you get for $4.50? How much will 54 tickets cost?

▲ Find common denominators. Add the fractions. Simplify to lowest terms.

1.
$$\frac{4}{7} + \frac{5}{6} =$$

2.
$$\frac{8}{9} + \frac{2}{3} =$$

3.
$$\frac{7}{10} + \frac{4}{5} =$$

4.
$$\frac{1}{2} + \frac{3}{4} =$$

5.
$$\frac{1}{6} + \frac{11}{12} =$$

6.
$$\frac{4}{9} + \frac{5}{12} =$$

▲ Find the average of each set of numbers.

1.   67   31   52   48   92

_____

2.   34,675   39,534   32,318

_____

3.   3,415   8,211   6,937   4,605

_____

4.   673   589   342   475   440   475

_____

5.   67,465   65,472   66,908

_____

6.   366   821   385   336

_____

▲ Add or subtract.

1.
```
   567.93
    63.721
+ 241.0085
```

2.
```
   3,627.9
 −3,617.874
```

3.
```
     2.635
   256.7289
+ 500.03706
```

4.
```
   0.0034
  35.728
+16.8396
```

Bonus Box: Use grid paper to sketch five different shapes with an area of 20. Find the perimeter of each.

Name _____

▲ Find common denominators. Add the fractions. Reduce to lowest terms.

1.
$$\frac{1}{3} + \frac{1}{2} + \frac{3}{4} =$$

2.
$$\frac{5}{6} + \frac{3}{4} + \frac{2}{3} =$$

3.
$$\frac{3}{8} + \frac{5}{6} + \frac{1}{3} =$$

4.
$$\frac{5}{9} + \frac{2}{3} + \frac{1}{6} =$$

5.
$$\frac{2}{5} + \frac{7}{10} + \frac{1}{4} =$$

6.
$$\frac{3}{7} + \frac{1}{2} + \frac{3}{4} =$$

▲ Find the mean, mode, median, and range for each set of numbers. Complete the chart.

Set A: 56   72   71   72   67   80   77   72   81

Set B: 14   21   17   23   17   21   17

Set C: 97   100   100   90   92   100   94   91

Set	Mean	Mode	Median	Range
A				
B				
C				

▲ Multiply or divide.

1.
$$\begin{array}{r} 8.09 \\ \times\ 3.1 \\ \hline \end{array}$$

2.
$$.56\overline{)22.288}$$

3.
$$.006\overline{).519}$$

4.
$$\begin{array}{r} 74.8 \\ \times\ .02 \\ \hline \end{array}$$

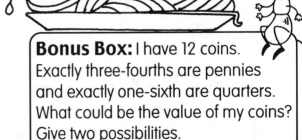

Bonus Box: I have 12 coins. Exactly three-fourths are pennies and exactly one-sixth are quarters. What could be the value of my coins? Give two possibilities.

Name _____

▲ Find common denominators. Subtract the fractions. Simplify to lowest terms.

1.
$$\frac{5}{6} - \frac{2}{3} =$$

2.
$$\frac{5}{8} - \frac{1}{4} =$$

3.
$$\frac{2}{3} - \frac{4}{7} =$$

4.
$$\frac{3}{5} - \frac{1}{3} =$$

5.
$$\frac{5}{9} - \frac{1}{6} =$$

6.
$$\frac{1}{2} - \frac{3}{8} =$$

▲ Find the mean, mode, median, and range for each set of numbers. Complete the chart.

Set A:	35	41	68	35	83			
Set B:	5	12	8	16	12	19		
Set C:	101	132	100	98	132	124	115	110	132

Set	Mean	Mode	Median	Range
A				
B				
C				

▲ Use the correct order of operations.

1. $6 \times (2 + 4) - 10 \div 2 =$ _____

2. $(6 + 10) \div 2 + 14 \div 2 =$ _____

3. $2 \times 5 + 3 \times 6 \div 9 =$ _____

4. $2 \times (2 + 1) - 10 \div (2 \times 5) =$ _____

5. $(10 - 8) \div 2 + (3 + 1) \times 4 =$ _____

6. $16 - 2 \times 2 + 8 \div 2 - 0 =$ _____

Bonus Box: Change the parentheses from the order of operations problems to obtain the following different answers. Change number 1 to equal 11. Change number 4 to equal 13.

Name _____

▲ Find common denominators. Subtract the fractions. Simplify to lowest terms.

1. $\dfrac{1}{2} - \dfrac{3}{7} =$

2. $\dfrac{7}{8} - \dfrac{3}{4} =$

3. $\dfrac{9}{10} - \dfrac{4}{5} =$

4. $\dfrac{4}{7} - \dfrac{1}{3} =$

5. $\dfrac{2}{3} - \dfrac{5}{9} =$

6. $\dfrac{4}{5} - \dfrac{1}{4} =$

▲ Find the mean, mode, median, and range for each set of numbers. Complete the chart.

Set A:	16	25	33	17	13	33
Set B:	68	74	99	51	68	
Set C:	88	87	89	90	85	88	89

Set	Mean	Mode	Median	Range
A				
B				
C				

▲ Write each decimal. Change each decimal to a percent. Change the percents to fractions. Write the fractions in simplest terms.

	Decimal	Percent	Fraction
1. eight hundredths	_____	_____	_____
2. forty hundredths	_____	_____	_____
3. sixty-five hundredths	_____	_____	_____
4. forty-two hundredths	_____	_____	_____

Bonus Box: On grid paper, sketch a figure that is 2 by 4 by 3. What is the volume of the figure? What is its surface area?

Name _____

▲ Find common denominators. Subtract the fractions. Simplify to lowest terms.

1.
$$\frac{3}{4} - \frac{2}{3} =$$

2.
$$\frac{7}{9} - \frac{2}{6} =$$

3.
$$\frac{4}{5} - \frac{2}{3} =$$

4.
$$\frac{7}{12} - \frac{2}{4} =$$

5.
$$\frac{1}{6} - \frac{1}{9} =$$

6.
$$\frac{4}{7} - \frac{2}{5} =$$

▲ Find the percentage.

1. 25% of 52 = _____

2. 33% of 300 = _____

3. 30% of 80 = _____

4. 2% of 400 = _____

5. 16% of 50 = _____

6. 62% of 50 = _____

▲ Find the volume of each figure.

1.
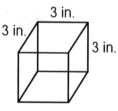
3 in.
3 in.
3 in.

_____ in.³

2.
5 cm
2 cm
3 cm

_____ cm³

3.
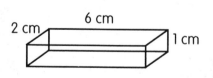
2 cm
6 cm
1 cm

_____ cm³

4.

2 m
2 m
7 m

_____ m³

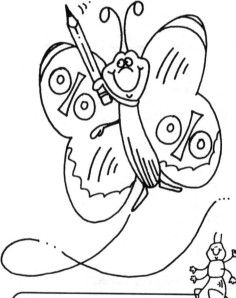

Bonus Box: Find the surface area for each of the four figures above.

▲ Find common denominators. Add the fractions. Simplify to lowest terms.

1.
$$2\,\frac{4}{5}$$
$$+\ 3\,\frac{2}{3}$$
_____

2.
$$4\,\frac{5}{6}$$
$$+\ 1\,\frac{3}{4}$$
_____

3.
$$1\,\frac{9}{10}$$
$$+\ 3\,\frac{3}{5}$$
_____

4.
$$4\,\frac{7}{8}$$
$$+\ 5\,\frac{1}{2}$$
_____

5.
$$5\,\frac{3}{4}$$
$$+\ 2\,\frac{5}{8}$$
_____

6.
$$3\,\frac{2}{5}$$
$$+\ 2\,\frac{3}{4}$$
_____

7.
$$2\,\frac{1}{2}$$
$$+\ 2\,\frac{6}{7}$$
_____

8.
$$4\,\frac{3}{4}$$
$$+\ 2\,\frac{2}{3}$$
_____

▲ Calculate the percentage.

1. 10% of 140 = _____

2. 21% of 100 = _____

3. 15% of 40 = _____

4. 55% of 60 = _____

5. 3% of 200 = _____

6. 80% of 5 = _____

▲ Add or subtract the integers. The first one is done for you.

1. −4 + +6 = ___+2___

2. −3 + −5 = _____

3. −9 + +2 = _____

4. +3 + −4 = _____

5. −4 − −2 = _____

6. −10 − +5 = _____

7. +6 − +8 = _____

8. +9 − −3 = _____

Bonus Box: Write five numbers with four digits each. The digits in each number have a sum of 18.

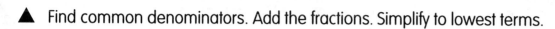

Name _____

▲ Find common denominators. Add the fractions. Simplify to lowest terms.

1.
$$4\frac{7}{8}$$
$$+ 1\frac{1}{2}$$
_____

2.
$$3\frac{4}{5}$$
$$+ 2\frac{5}{6}$$
_____

3.
$$8\frac{1}{2}$$
$$+ 1\frac{5}{7}$$
_____

4.
$$1\frac{9}{10}$$
$$+ 6\frac{1}{2}$$
_____

5.
$$2\frac{11}{12}$$
$$+ 3\frac{3}{4}$$
_____

6.
$$1\frac{7}{9}$$
$$+ 3\frac{5}{6}$$
_____

7.
$$4\frac{3}{4}$$
$$+ 3\frac{1}{2}$$
_____

8.
$$1\frac{4}{7}$$
$$+ 2\frac{2}{5}$$
_____

▲ Calculate the percentage.

1. 5% of 140 = _____

2. 34% of 200 = _____

3. 90% of 60 = _____

4. 14% of 150 = _____

5. 8% of 25 = _____

6. 70% of 20 = _____

▲ Add or subtract the integers.

1. −9 − +3 = _____

2. +4 − + 8 = _____

3. +2 + −7 = _____

4. +8 − −10 = _____

5. −12 − −4 = _____

6. −4 − +12 = _____

7. −9 − −15 = _____

8. +1 + +3 = _____

9. +13 − −2 = _____

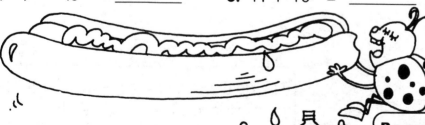

Bonus Box: Show at least five ways to make $5.21 using coins.

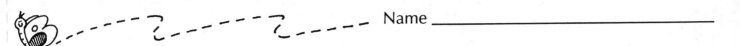

Name _____

▲ Find common denominators. Add the fractions. Simplify to lowest terms.

1.
$$2\frac{1}{4}$$
$$+\ 1\frac{2}{3}$$
_____

2.
$$6\frac{7}{8}$$
$$+\ 3\frac{1}{4}$$
_____

3.
$$2\frac{7}{10}$$
$$+\ 4\frac{3}{4}$$
_____

4.
$$2\frac{4}{5}$$
$$+\ 1\frac{1}{2}$$
_____

5.
$$3\frac{4}{7}$$
$$+\ 2\frac{1}{2}$$
_____

6.
$$2\frac{1}{3}$$
$$+\ 3\frac{7}{9}$$
_____

7.
$$1\frac{2}{3}$$
$$+\ 5\frac{5}{8}$$
_____

8.
$$2\frac{4}{9}$$
$$+\ 4\frac{5}{6}$$
_____

▲ There are three ways to write ratios: 5 to 6, 5/6, or 5:6. Write each ratio two other ways.

1. 2 to 3   _____ _____

2. 9 to 6   _____ _____

3. _____   7/3   _____

4. _____   5/9   _____

5. _____   _____   3:6

6. _____   _____   8:4

7. 12 to 9   _____ _____

8. 1 to 7   _____ _____

9. _____   _____   8:3

10. _____   12/5   _____

▲ Add or subtract the integers.

1. –12 + +5 = _____

2. +14 – +13 = _____

3. –8 + –12 = _____

4. –8 – –11 = _____

5. –2 – +7 = _____

6. +10 + –6 = _____

7. +2 + +4 = _____

8. –15 + +14 = _____

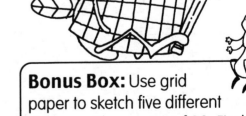

Bonus Box: Use grid paper to sketch five different shapes with an area of 30. Find the perimeter of each.

Name _____

▲ Find common denominators. Subtract the fractions. Simplify to lowest terms.

1.
$3\dfrac{1}{5}$
$-\ 1\dfrac{1}{2}$

2.
$6\dfrac{1}{3}$
$-\ 4\dfrac{7}{9}$

3.
$4\dfrac{5}{9}$
$-\ 1\dfrac{3}{4}$

4.
$8\dfrac{1}{2}$
$-\ 5\dfrac{6}{7}$

5.
$7\dfrac{2}{6}$
$-\ 2\dfrac{7}{12}$

6.
$9\dfrac{3}{10}$
$-\ 4\dfrac{5}{6}$

7.
$5\dfrac{1}{4}$
$-\ 1\dfrac{7}{8}$

8.
$2\dfrac{4}{9}$
$-\ 1\dfrac{5}{6}$

▲ There are three ways to write ratios: 5 to 6, 5/6, or 5:6. Write each ratio two other ways.

1. 6 to 1 _____ _____

2. 14 to 3 _____ _____

3. _____ 4/7 _____

4. _____ 2/9 _____

5. _____ _____ 6:11

6. _____ _____ 8:3

7. 15 to 4 _____ _____

8. 2 to 10 _____ _____

9. _____ _____ 24:19

10. _____ 51/18 _____

▲ Write the algebraic expression for each word expression. The first one is done for you.

1. r decreased by 4

____**r−4**____

2. y divided by 2

_____

3. p and 7

_____

4. d times 3

_____

5. 12 divided by g

_____

6. 5 less than k

_____

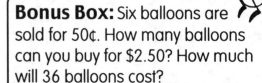

Bonus Box: Six balloons are sold for 50¢. How many balloons can you buy for $2.50? How much will 36 balloons cost?

Name _____

▲ Find common denominators. Subtract the fractions. Simplify to lowest terms.

1.
$$5\frac{1}{2}$$
$$-2\frac{5}{6}$$

2.
$$4\frac{2}{5}$$
$$-2\frac{7}{10}$$

3.
$$7\frac{1}{9}$$
$$-3\frac{5}{6}$$

4.
$$6\frac{1}{8}$$
$$-1\frac{2}{6}$$

5.
$$3\frac{3}{10}$$
$$-2\frac{1}{2}$$

6.
$$8\frac{1}{3}$$
$$-3\frac{5}{9}$$

7.
$$9\frac{4}{7}$$
$$-1\frac{3}{4}$$

8.
$$4\frac{1}{6}$$
$$-2\frac{5}{9}$$

▲ Draw a model of each ratio.

1. The ratio of red cubes to blue cubes is 3 to 7.

2. The ratio of subtraction problems to addition problems is 4:1.

3. The ratio of total books to biographies is 5:2.

4. The ratio of boys to girls is 1/3.

▲ Write the algebraic expression for each word expression. The first one is done for you.

1. 5 more than y

   $y + 5$

2. 16 minus r

   _____

3. 10 divided by p

   _____

4. 6 times z

   _____

5. m divided by 3

   _____

6. 4 more than b

   _____

Bonus Box: Sketch two three-dimensional figures. Label the dimensions. Give the volume and surface area for each figure.

Name _____

▲ Find common denominators. Subtract the fractions. Simplify to lowest terms.

1.
$$5\frac{4}{7}$$
$$-2\frac{2}{3}$$

2.
$$7\frac{1}{4}$$
$$-4\frac{1}{3}$$

3.
$$9\frac{1}{10}$$
$$-1\frac{1}{2}$$

4.
$$4\frac{1}{3}$$
$$-2\frac{3}{5}$$

5.
$$2\frac{3}{7}$$
$$-\frac{3}{4}$$

6.
$$8\frac{1}{9}$$
$$-1\frac{1}{3}$$

7.
$$7\frac{2}{5}$$
$$-2\frac{1}{2}$$

8.
$$4\frac{5}{12}$$
$$-3\frac{5}{6}$$

▲ Draw a model of each ratio.

1. The ratio of striped socks to solid-colored socks is 2:6.

2. The ratio of total dots to green dots is 9 to 2.

3. The ratio of candy bars to suckers is 10/1.

4. The ratio of yellow pencils to total pencils is 5:6.

▲ Write the word expression for each algebraic expression.

1. $6 - g$ _____

2. $4h$ _____

3. $f + 3$ _____

4. $r/5$ _____

5. $p - 14$ _____

6. $4/y$ _____

Bonus Box: Write five number sentences with an answer of $4\frac{1}{3}$.

Name _____

▲ Find common denominators. Add or subtract the fractions. Simplify to lowest terms.

1.
$$2\frac{4}{5}$$
$$+\ 3\frac{7}{10}$$

2.
$$6\frac{1}{2}$$
$$-\ 1\frac{5}{6}$$

3.
$$4\frac{2}{3}$$
$$+\ 2\frac{5}{9}$$

4.
$$6\frac{3}{8}$$
$$-\ 2\frac{3}{4}$$

5.
$$9\frac{5}{7}$$
$$-\ 4\frac{2}{3}$$

6.
$$2\frac{3}{4}$$
$$+\ 1\frac{5}{6}$$

7.
$$5\frac{2}{9}$$
$$-\ 1\frac{5}{6}$$

8.
$$4\frac{1}{2}$$
$$-\ 2\frac{8}{9}$$

▲ Circle each set of equivalent ratios. If they are not equivalent, change the second ratio to make them equivalent.

1. 4 to 5   8 to 10   **2.** 6:2   12:4   **3.** 12/5   6/3

4. 3:8   9:24   **5.** 7/2   14/3   **6.** 10 to 3 30 to 9

7. 5/11   15/22   **8.** 4 to 8 1 to 2   **9.** 36:6   6:2

▲ Write the word expression for each algebraic expression.

1. t4 _____

2. 5 + h _____

3. r/5 _____

4. w6 _____

5. q+2 _____

6. 44/f _____

Bonus Box: Write five numbers that have six digits each so that the sum of the digits for each number is 38, the first digit is greater than the second digit, and no digit is zero.

   IF87123 • Mixed Skills in Math 5-6

▲ Find common denominators. Add or subtract the fractions. Simplify to lowest terms.

1.
$$4\frac{6}{7}$$
$$+\,5\frac{1}{2}$$

2.
$$4\frac{2}{3}$$
$$-\,2\frac{7}{9}$$

3.
$$8\frac{1}{5}$$
$$+\,2\frac{2}{3}$$

4.
$$3\frac{5}{8}$$
$$+\,3\frac{3}{4}$$

5.
$$5\frac{1}{2}$$
$$-\,2\frac{7}{8}$$

6.
$$1\frac{3}{4}$$
$$+\,1\frac{5}{6}$$

7.
$$3\frac{4}{9}$$
$$-\,1\frac{5}{6}$$

8.
$$6\frac{1}{10}$$
$$-\,2\frac{1}{2}$$

▲ Circle each set of equivalent ratios. If they are not equivalent, change the second ratio to make them equivalent.

1. 5:6   15:12

2. 3/1   9/3

3. 4 to 7   12 to 17

4. 6/2   4/1

5. 9 to 3   30 to 10

6. 8:5   40:25

7. 2:6   1:4

8. 15/6   5/3

9. 1 to 4   4 to 16

▲ Solve each algebraic expression for the given values. The first one has been done for you.

1. Solve $2g$
   if $g = 2.45$ ___**4.9**___   if $g = 34$ _____   if $g = 0.086$ _____

2. Solve $h - 3.465$
   if $h = 4.02$ _____   if $h = 56$ _____   if $h = 6.3$ _____

Bonus Box: Twelve coins are in a bank. Exactly one-half are pennies, and exactly one-third are nickels. What could be the value of the coins in the bank? Provide two possibilities.

Name _____

▲ Find the products. Simplify to lowest terms. The first one is done for you.

1. $\dfrac{1}{3} \times \dfrac{6}{7} = \dfrac{6}{21} = \dfrac{2}{7}$

2. $\dfrac{2}{5} \times \dfrac{15}{16} =$

3. $\dfrac{5}{6} \times \dfrac{3}{5} =$

4. $\dfrac{4}{9} \times \dfrac{3}{4} =$

▲ Refer to the table to calculate the relative frequency of each event. Write as a ratio. The first one is done for you.

What is the relative frequency of . . .

Purchases at Movie Night

Grade	Popcorn	Trail Mix	# of Students
Fifth	70	25	95
Sixth	30	50	80
Seventh	45	55	100

1. a sixth grader purchasing trail mix?
50:80

2. a fifth grader purchasing popcorn?
_____

3. a seventh grader purchasing trail mix? _____

4. a fifth or seventh grader purchasing popcorn? _____

5. a sixth or seventh grader purchasing trail mix? _____

6. a fifth, sixth, or seventh grader purchasing popcorn? _____

▲ Solve each algebraic expression for the given values.

1. Solve r ÷ 2.2
if r = 79.2 _____   if r = 3.3 _____   if r = 100.54 _____

2. Solve w + 23.65
if w = 21.35 _____   if w = 45.77 _____   if w = 0.899 _____

Bonus Box: Four mugs are sold for $3.00. How many mugs can you buy for $12.00? How much will 36 mugs cost?

▲ Find the products. Simplify to lowest terms.

1. $\frac{2}{3} \times \frac{9}{10} =$ _____

2. $\frac{5}{6} \times \frac{3}{10} =$ _____

3. $\frac{2}{5} \times \frac{10}{11} =$ _____

4. $\frac{4}{9} \times \frac{6}{7} =$ _____

5. $\frac{1}{12} \times \frac{3}{4} =$ _____

6. $\frac{1}{7} \times \frac{2}{5} =$ _____

▲ Refer to the table to calculate the relative frequency of each event. Write as a ratio.

Favorite Writing Tools

Grade	Pens	Pencils	Markers	Colored Pencils
Fifth	36	52	22	10
Sixth	41	53	11	25
Seventh	63	65	20	12

What is the relative frequency of a . . .

1. seventh grader prefering markers?
_____

2. fifth or sixth grader prefering pencils?
_____

3. fifth grader prefering pencils or pens?
_____

4. sixth or seventh grader prefering pens or markers? _____

5. sixth grader prefering markers or colored pencils? _____

6. fifth, sixth, or seventh grader prefering pens? _____

▲ Solve each algebraic expression for the given values.

1. $79.2 + u =$ _____
$u = 0.87$

2. $8a =$ _____
$a = 2.6$

3. $3\frac{5}{6} + n =$ _____
$n = 1\frac{2}{3}$

4. $y/9 =$ _____
$y = 40.5$

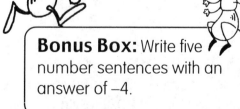

Bonus Box: Write five number sentences with an answer of –4.

Name _____

▲ Find the products. Simplify to lowest terms.

1. $3 \times \dfrac{2}{3} =$

2. $\dfrac{4}{5} \times \dfrac{1}{3} =$

3. $\dfrac{3}{7} \times 2 =$

4. $\dfrac{24}{25} \times \dfrac{5}{8} =$

5. $8 \times \dfrac{3}{8} =$

6. $\dfrac{3}{4} \times \dfrac{10}{12} =$

▲ Refer to the table to calculate the probability of each event. Write as a ratio.

Study Time Preferences at Lakeshore School

Grade	Before School	Study Hall	After School	Evening
Fifth	16	82	51	41
Sixth	29	55	54	62
Seventh	31	84	42	53

What is the probability that a . . .

1. sixth grader prefers studying before school? _____

2. sixth or seventh grader prefers studying in study hall? _____

3. fifth grader prefers studying in the evening? _____

4. fifth or seventh grader prefers studying after school? _____

5. seventh grader prefers studying after school or in the evening? _____

6. fifth, sixth, or seventh grader prefers studying before school or in the evening? _____

▲ Solve each algebraic expression for the given values.

1. $k + \dfrac{4}{5} =$ _____

$k = \dfrac{2}{3}$

2. $9/p =$ _____

$p = 45$

3. $z - 2\dfrac{3}{4} =$ _____

$z = 6\dfrac{1}{8}$

4. $2t =$ _____

$t = \dfrac{9}{10}$

Bonus Box: Use the data in the table above to write five probability statements with answers.

▲ Find the products. Simplify to lowest terms.

1. $\dfrac{1}{4} \times 2 =$

2. $\dfrac{2}{5} \times \dfrac{5}{6} =$

3. $\dfrac{4}{7} \times \dfrac{3}{8} =$

4. $\dfrac{3}{4} \times \dfrac{1}{2} =$

5. $\dfrac{14}{21} \times \dfrac{7}{14} =$

6. $\dfrac{2}{3} \times \dfrac{5}{8} =$

▲ Refer to the tree diagrams of possible combinations of doughnut topping choices.

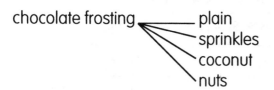

chocolate frosting —— plain
sprinkles
coconut
nuts

vanilla frosting —— plain
sprinkles
coconut
nuts

What is the probability of having a doughnut with . . .

1. chocolate frosting and nuts? ___**1:8**___

2. plain frosting? _____

3. frosting with sprinkles? _____

4. chocolate frosting and coconut or nuts? _____

5. vanilla frosting with coconut, nuts, or sprinkles? _____

6. cherry frosting with sprinkles? _____

▲ Solve each algebraic expression for the given values.

1. $4.2b =$ _____
  $b = 5.67$

2. $\dfrac{1}{3} + s =$ _____
  $s = \dfrac{3}{4}$

3. $w/0.23 =$ _____
  $w = 0.92$

4. $2\dfrac{4}{5} - k =$ _____
  $k = \dfrac{11}{10}$

Bonus Box: Six doughnuts sell for $1.50. How many doughnuts can you buy for $9.00? How much will four dozen doughnuts cost?

Name _____

▲ Find the quotients. Simplify to lowest terms. The first one is done for you.

1. $\dfrac{1}{2} \div \dfrac{3}{4} =$

$\dfrac{1}{2} \times \dfrac{4}{3} = \dfrac{4}{6} = \mathbf{\dfrac{2}{3}}$

2. $\dfrac{3}{5} \div \dfrac{6}{7} =$

3. $\dfrac{2}{9} \div \dfrac{4}{6} =$

4. $\dfrac{1}{10} \div \dfrac{2}{5} =$

▲ Draw tree diagrams to illustrate possible combinations of two chores at Sally's house.

Choose one dinner chore:
  wash dishes
  dry dishes
  set table
  clear table

Choose one cleaning chore:
  vacuum
  dust
  sweep
  windows

What is the probability of choosing . . .

1. to wash dishes and dust or vacuum?
  _____

2. to set or clear the table and vacuum or sweep? _____

3. to wash the windows? _____

4. to set the table? _____

5. to set the table and dust or do windows? _____

6. wash or dry dishes and sweep?
  _____

▲ Solve for each letter.

1. $h - \dfrac{5}{6} = 1\dfrac{1}{3}$

  h = _____

2. $3.5 - p = 1.017$

  p = _____

3. s/4 = 62

  s = _____

4. $\dfrac{1}{2}n = \dfrac{2}{5}$

  n = _____

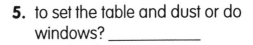

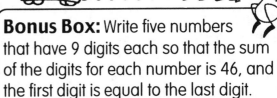

Bonus Box: Write five numbers that have 9 digits each so that the sum of the digits for each number is 46, and the first digit is equal to the last digit.

Name _____

▲ Find the quotients. Simplify to lowest terms.

1. $\dfrac{4}{5} \div \dfrac{2}{7} =$

2. $\dfrac{1}{9} \div \dfrac{5}{6} =$

3. $\dfrac{2}{9} \div \dfrac{1}{12} =$

4. $\dfrac{3}{10} \div \dfrac{9}{14} =$

5. $\dfrac{1}{2} \div \dfrac{7}{8} =$

6. $\dfrac{4}{7} \div \dfrac{2}{3} =$

▲ Draw tree diagrams to illustrate the possible combinations of project choices. Each student must make one choice from each column.

written report	diorama	oral presentation
chapter questions	poster	movement presentation
	game	multimedia presentation
	book	

What is the probability of choosing . . .

1. the written report? _____

2. the game? _____

3. the oral presentation? _____

4. the chapter questions and a movement presentation? _____

5. the diorama and a multimedia presentation? _____

6. the written report, a book, and an oral presentation? _____

▲ Solve for each letter.

1. $\dfrac{2}{5} \div g = \dfrac{7}{10}$

g = _____

2. r – 1,463 = 837

r = _____

3. e/2.2 = 89.1

e = _____

4. b0.62 = 26.598

b = _____

5. $\dfrac{2}{3} + c + \dfrac{4}{9} = 1\dfrac{5}{18}$

c = _____

6. $4\dfrac{1}{2} - f = 3\dfrac{1}{8}$

f = _____

Bonus Box: Sketch four rectangles. Label the length of each side. Find the perimeter and area of each figure.

▲ Find the quotients. Simplify to lowest terms.

1.
$$\frac{4}{9} \div \frac{12}{27} =$$

2.
$$\frac{5}{12} \div \frac{1}{6} =$$

3.
$$\frac{2}{7} \div \frac{4}{9} =$$

4.
$$\frac{2}{3} \div \frac{4}{9} =$$

5.
$$\frac{7}{10} \div \frac{3}{5} =$$

6.
$$\frac{1}{8} \div \frac{3}{4} =$$

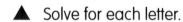

▲ There are 5 blue cubes, 8 purple cubes, and 7 white cubes in a box. Write the probability of choosing . . .

1. a blue cube. _____

2. a red cube. _____

3. a purple marble. _____

4. a purple cube. _____

5. a white cube. _____

If you return the cube to the bag each time, what is the probability of choosing . . .

1. a white cube if you make 100 picks?_____

2. a blue or purple cube if you make 40 picks? _____

▲ Solve for each letter.

1. $3.06 + m + 39.682 = 67.213$ $m =$ _____

2. $.09s = 3.852$ $s =$ _____

3. $k - 1.6429 = 0.4571$ $k =$ _____

4. $325.89/p = 5.1$ $p =$ _____

5. $t + 274,809 = 744,047$ $t =$ _____

6. $8.3a = 18.758$ $a =$ _____

Bonus Box: Show at least five ways to make $2.61 using coins.

▲ Find the quotients. Simplify to lowest terms.

1. $\dfrac{6}{7} \div \dfrac{2}{3} =$

2. $\dfrac{5}{9} \div \dfrac{7}{12} =$

3. $\dfrac{4}{7} \div \dfrac{2}{5} =$

4. $\dfrac{3}{4} \div \dfrac{15}{16} =$

5. $\dfrac{1}{9} \div \dfrac{2}{15} =$

6. $\dfrac{9}{10} \div \dfrac{12}{15} =$

▲ There are 3 hot-pink sunglasses, 15 navy-blue sunglasses, 12 cherry-red sunglasses, and 8 sunshine-yellow sunglasses in a box. What is the probability of choosing . . .

1. navy-blue sunglasses? _____

2. cherry-red or sunshine-yellow sunglasses? _____

3. forest-green sunglasses? _____

4. hot-pink sunglasses? _____

5. sunshine-yellow, hot-pink, or navy-blue sunglasses? _____

If you return the sunglasses to the box each time, what is the probability of choosing . . .

1. hot-pink sunglasses if you make 228 picks?_____

2. navy-blue or cherry-red sunglasses if you make 152 picks? _____

▲ Solve for each letter.

$s = (m + n)(j - k)$

$m + m = j$

$n + n = m$

$n + k = 5$

$k - n = 1$

s = _____ m = _____ n = _____

j = _____ k = _____

Bonus Box: Find and trace 12 angles. Find 3 obtuse angles, 3 right angles, and 3 acute angles. Label each and write where you found each.

▲ Multiply or divide. Simplify to lowest terms.

1. $\frac{4}{5} \times \frac{1}{6} =$

2. $\frac{8}{9} \times \frac{3}{7} =$

3. $\frac{14}{25} \times \frac{5}{7} =$

4. $\frac{2}{3} \div \frac{4}{9} =$

5. $\frac{3}{4} \div \frac{9}{10} =$

6. $\frac{7}{8} \div \frac{1}{4} =$

▲ There are 12 mint, 15 toffee, 10 caramel, and 14 chocolate candies in a bag. What is the probability of choosing . . .

1. a mint candy? _____

2. a chocolate candy? _____

3. a toffee or caramel candy? _____

4. a coconut candy? _____

5. a mint, chocolate, or toffee candy? _____

If you return the candy to the box each time, what is the probability of choosing . . .

1. a caramel candy if you make 357 picks? _____

2. a chocolate or caramel candy if you make 152 picks? _____

▲ Solve for each letter.

$b + c = d + c + e - 9$

$c + 1 = d$

$2d = e$

$e - b = c$

$c - 3 = 8 - 7$

b = _____ c = _____ d = _____

e = _____

Bonus Box: Four ounces of cleaner is needed for 3 quarts of water. How many ounces of cleaner are needed for 21 quarts of water? How much water is needed for 16 ounces of cleaner?

Name _____

▲ Multiply. Simplify to lowest terms. The first one is done for you.

1.
$$3 \times \frac{4}{3} = \frac{12}{3} \text{ or } \mathbf{4}$$

2.
$$\frac{5}{8} \times 12 =$$

3.
$$\frac{4}{5} \times 10 =$$

4.
$$6 \times \frac{1}{4} =$$

5.
$$\frac{5}{6} \times 8 =$$

6.
$$3 \times \frac{4}{9} =$$

▲ Use the spinner to determine the probability of each event.

What is the probability of the spinner . . .

1. stopping on an 8? _____

2. stopping on a number less than 14? _____

3. stopping on a number greater than or equal to 6? _____

4. stopping on an even number? _____

5. stopping on an odd number? _____

6. stopping on 6, 8, 10, 14, or 16? _____

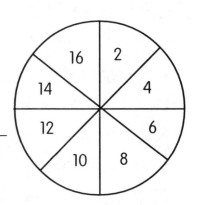

▲ Room 34 recorded on a stem-and-leaf plot the passing scores for a science project. Use the stem-and-leaf plot to answer the questions.

Passing Scores

9	0 0 2 3 4 7 8
8	0 0 1 1 1 1 5 7 7 7 9
7	4 6 7 7 8 9
6	7 8 9 9

1. Which score occurred most often? _____

2. How many students had passing scores? _____

3. If there are 35 people in the class, how many students did not have a passing grade? _____

4. A score of 78 to 86 is a "B." How many students received a "B"? _____

5. What is the probability that Cia earned a "B" for her project grade? _____

Bonus Box: Write five numbers with ten digits each so that the sum of the digits for each number is less than 30, and the digit in the tenths place is 4.

Name _____

▲ Multiply. Simplify to lowest terms. The first one is done for you.

1.
$5\frac{1}{4} \times 2\frac{2}{7} = $ **12**

2.
$1\frac{7}{9} \times 4\frac{1}{2} = $

3.
$3\frac{1}{3} \times 1\frac{1}{2} = $

4.
$3\frac{3}{5} \times \frac{2}{9} = $

5.
$1\frac{5}{7} \times \frac{5}{6} = $

6.
$\frac{3}{7} \times 5\frac{1}{4} = $

▲ Match the words with the definitions.

_____ **1.** acute triangle

_____ **2.** octagon

_____ **3.** triangle

_____ **4.** trapezoid

_____ **5.** parallelogram

a. a closed figure with three sides and three vertices

b. a quadrilateral with one set of parallel sides

c. a triangle with one angle that is less than 90°

d. a quadrilateral with opposite sides that are parallel

e. a polygon with 8 sides and 8 vertices

▲ For three weeks, William recorded his heart rate after running one mile. Use the stem-and-leaf plot to answer the questions.

Heart rate

17	0 2 2 3 4 4 5 7
16	3 5 5 5 5 7 8
15	1 3 8 8 9

1. Which heart rate occurred most often? _____

2. What are the heart rates shown by the first stem and
its leaves? _____

3. What is the mode? _____

4. What is the median heart rate? _____

5. Which heart rate occurred more often, 158 or 167?

_____

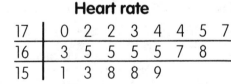

Bonus Box: Use the data in
the stem-and-leaf plot to make a
bar graph.

▲ Multiply. Reduce to lowest terms.

1.
$$3\frac{1}{3} \times 2\frac{1}{4} =$$

2.
$$2\frac{2}{5} \times \frac{2}{9} =$$

3.
$$6\frac{2}{3} \times 2\frac{1}{4} =$$

4.
$$2\frac{3}{4} \times 2\frac{2}{3} =$$

5.
$$2\frac{1}{7} \times 2\frac{4}{5} =$$

6.
$$10\frac{1}{2} \times 3\frac{1}{3} =$$

▲ Match the words with the definitions.

_____ **1.** quadrilateral   **a.** a polygon with 6 sides and 6 vertices

_____ **2.** right triangle   **b.** a triangle with one 90° angle

_____ **3.** hexagon   **c.** a polygon with 4 sides and 4 vertices

_____ **4.** pentagon   **d.** a triangle with one angle that is greater than 90°

_____ **5.** obtuse triangle   **e.** a polygon with 5 sides and 5 vertices

▲ Use the following data to make a stem-and-leaf plot. Then use the stem-and-leaf plot to answer the questions.

Numbers

Data

18	10	24	30	41	42
31	18	27	33	40	43
27	37	15	39	27	43
17	36	26	16	41	40

4 _____

3 _____

2 _____

1 _____

1. What numbers are shown by the first stem and its leaves? _____

2. What is the mode? _____

3. What is the median? _____

4. What is the range? _____

Bonus Box: Sketch each of the geometric figures described above.

Name _____

▲ Multiply. Simplify to lowest terms.

1.
$5 \dfrac{2}{6} \times 2 \dfrac{2}{8} =$

2.
$4 \dfrac{6}{9} \times 6 \dfrac{3}{4} =$

3.
$5 \dfrac{1}{3} \times \dfrac{1}{16} =$

4.
$3 \dfrac{1}{3} \times 2 \dfrac{1}{4} =$

5.
$2 \dfrac{2}{9} \times 1 \dfrac{1}{5} =$

6.
$2 \dfrac{3}{6} \times \dfrac{9}{10} =$

▲ Write the numeral for each number word.

1. Seven billion, ten thousand, four and six tenths _____

2. Fifty-eight million, two hundred thousand, sixty-five and fifteen hundredths

_____

3. Seventy-nine and five thousandths

_____

4. Nine hundred sixty-one billion, one hundred million, seven hundred twenty-four

_____

5. Six and forty-five ten thousandths

_____

▲ Add or subtract.

1.
$$\begin{array}{r} 50{,}000{,}000 \\ -\ 23{,}089{,}702 \\ \hline \end{array}$$

2.
$$\begin{array}{r} 400{,}000 \\ -\ 39{,}002 \\ \hline \end{array}$$

3.
$$\begin{array}{r} 56{,}873{,}298 \\ +\ 25{,}361{,}345 \\ \hline \end{array}$$

4.
$$\begin{array}{r} 90{,}003{,}000 \\ -\ 21{,}345{,}321 \\ \hline \end{array}$$

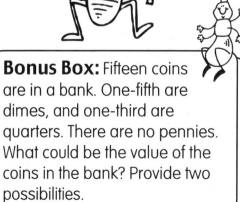

Bonus Box: Fifteen coins are in a bank. One-fifth are dimes, and one-third are quarters. There are no pennies. What could be the value of the coins in the bank? Provide two possibilities.

▲ Divide. Simplify to lowest terms.

1.
$$4 \frac{2}{3} \div \frac{8}{9} =$$

2.
$$3 \frac{3}{6} \div 4 \frac{2}{3} =$$

3.
$$1 \frac{1}{7} \div 1 \frac{3}{7} =$$

4.
$$1 \frac{7}{8} \div 7 \frac{2}{4} =$$

5.
$$1 \frac{5}{9} \div 3 \frac{1}{3} =$$

6.
$$3 \frac{9}{10} \div 1 \frac{4}{5} =$$

▲ Round . . .

1. to the nearest hundred thousand.

456,736,225,142   56,950,382,001   156,723,645.2573

_____   _____   _____

2. to the nearest hundredth.

352,637.84328   10.08923   9,452,367.1623

_____   _____   _____

3. to the nearest ten million.

34,526,738,901.223   245,174,838.5562   321,234,683

_____   _____   _____

▲ Add.

1.	**2.**	**3.**
8,352,716	601,231	1,002,573
1,023,637	235,637	4,341,734
425,673	24,601	83,261
2,115	34,256	5,372
+ 41	+ 1,617	+ 709

Bonus Box: Write four numbers that when rounded to the nearest ten thousand, round to 432,156,280,000. Include numbers that round up and numbers that round down.

Name _____

▲ Divide. Simplify to lowest terms.

1.
$2 \dfrac{2}{8} \div 6 \dfrac{3}{4} =$

2.
$5 \dfrac{5}{8} \div 2 \dfrac{3}{16} =$

3.
$6 \dfrac{2}{9} \div 3 \dfrac{3}{6} =$

4.
$7 \dfrac{1}{5} \div 30 =$

5.
$2 \dfrac{3}{6} \div 2 \dfrac{2}{9} =$

6.
$2 \dfrac{4}{5} \div 2 \dfrac{1}{10} =$

▲ Find the perimeter of each figure.

1.
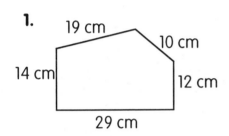
19 cm
10 cm
14 cm
12 cm
29 cm

_____ **cm**

2.
63 in.
28 in.

_____ **in.**

3.
4 m
5 m
7 m

_____ **m**

▲ Multiply or divide.

1.
623
$\times\ 54$

2.
$47 \overline{\smash{)}18{,}706}$

3.
$73 \overline{\smash{)}67{,}671}$

4.
296
$\times\ 37$

5.
$61 \overline{\smash{)}34{,}953}$

6.
$28 \overline{\smash{)}19{,}460}$

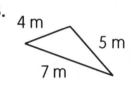

Bonus Box: Use grid paper to sketch five different shapes with an area of 22 square units. Find the perimeter of each.

Name _____

▲ Divide. Simplify to lowest terms.

1.
$1 \frac{7}{15} \div 2 \frac{4}{5} =$

2.
$1 \frac{13}{14} \div 1 \frac{5}{7} =$

3.
$1 \frac{7}{8} \div \frac{9}{32} =$

4.
$3 \frac{3}{14} \div 2 \frac{4}{7} =$

5.
$3 \frac{3}{6} \div 5 \frac{5}{6} =$

6.
$2 \frac{6}{7} \div 2 \frac{2}{14} =$

▲ Use the correct order of operations.

1. $(2 - 1) \times (3 + 6) =$

2. $(46 - 6) \div (2 + 1 \times 2) =$

3. $21 \div 7 + (2 + 6) \times 4 =$

4. $(2 + 10 - 3) \div (1 + 2) =$

5. $(6 + 24 \div 6) \div 5 =$

6. $10 \times 6 \div (3 + 5 + 2) =$

▲ Add or subtract.

1.
$$4.28998$$
$$31.4972$$
$$+ \ 0.19213$$

2.
$$53.67$$
$$- \ 49.25734$$

3.
$$9.004$$
$$- \ 5.83241$$

4.
$$63.208$$
$$412.52$$
$$+ \ 98.3522$$

Bonus Box: Change problem number 2 from the order of operations activity to equal 45. Change number 2 to equal 42.

Name _____

▲ Divide. Simplify to lowest terms.

1. $2\dfrac{4}{5} \div 2\dfrac{1}{10} =$

2. $1\dfrac{1}{3} \div 1\dfrac{13}{27} =$

3. $3\dfrac{3}{4} \div 1\dfrac{7}{18} =$

4. $3\dfrac{1}{3} \div \dfrac{14}{27} =$

5. $3\dfrac{3}{5} \div 1\dfrac{1}{15} =$

6. $1\dfrac{1}{5} \div 2\dfrac{2}{5} =$

▲ Find the mean, mode, median, and range for each set of numbers. Complete the chart.

Set A:	5	7	5	9	6	5	5	8	4
Set B:	26	30	42	55	63	50			
Set C:	2	93	46	4	16	4	99		

Set	Mean	Mode	Median	Range
A				
B				
C				

▲ Multiply or divide.

1. $.018\overline{)5.274}$

2. $.74\overline{)11.988}$

3. $\begin{array}{r} 98.2 \\ \times\ 7.8 \\ \hline \end{array}$

4. $\begin{array}{r} 42.9 \\ \times 6.2 \\ \hline \end{array}$

Bonus Box: You can buy four tadpoles for $0.66. How many tadpoles can you get for $4.62? How much will 36 tadpoles cost?

▲ Multiply or divide. Simplify to lowest terms.

1.
$$1 \frac{1}{15} \div 2 \frac{2}{3} =$$

2.
$$1 \frac{1}{14} \times 2 \frac{1}{10} =$$

3.
$$2 \frac{12}{15} \div 7 \frac{1}{5} =$$

4.
$$3 \frac{3}{4} \times 1 \frac{1}{5} =$$

5.
$$1 \frac{1}{5} \times 1 \frac{3}{12} =$$

6.
$$\frac{8}{21} \div 1 \frac{5}{7} =$$

▲ Write each decimal. Change each decimal to a percent. Change the percents to fractions. Write the fractions in lowest terms.

	Decimal	Percent	Fraction
1. twenty hundredths			
2. fifty-five hundredths			
3. thirty-eight hundredths			
4. eight hundredths			
5. ninety-two hundredths			
6. fifteen hundredths			

▲ Add or subtract the integers.

1. $-7 - +4 =$

2. $-3 + -5 =$

3. $+4 + +7 =$

4. $-7 + -9 =$

5. $-16 - +1 =$

6. $-14 - -17 =$

7. $+2 + -10 =$

8. $-12 + +9 =$

Bonus Box: Write five number sentences with an answer of –8.

▲ Multiply and divide. Simplify to lowest terms.

1. $1\frac{1}{9} \div 1\frac{1}{3} =$

2. $1\frac{1}{5} \div 2\frac{2}{5} =$

3. $5\frac{1}{4} \times 1\frac{1}{7} =$

4. $2\frac{2}{5} \times 1\frac{1}{14} =$

5. $2\frac{1}{7} \div 4\frac{2}{7} =$

6. $1\frac{1}{9} \div \frac{1}{9} =$

▲ Refer to the table to calculate the relative frequency of each event. Write as a ratio.

Seventh-Hour Class Choices

Grade	Rockets	Chemistry	Drama	Sculpture
Fifth	25	28	22	30
Sixth	34	26	45	15
Seventh	52	39	8	31

What is the relative frequency of a . . .

1. seventh grader taking drama?
_____

2. fifth or sixth grader taking rockets?
_____

3. fifth grader taking rockets or chemistry? _____

4. sixth or seventh grader taking drama or chemistry? _____

5. sixth grader taking drama or sculpture? _____

6. fifth, sixth, or seventh grader taking chemistry? _____

▲ Solve each algebraic expression for the given values.

1. $6.2 + k =$ _____
$k = 4.97$

2. $\frac{1}{3}s =$ _____
$s = 12$

3. $3\frac{1}{3} - p =$ _____
$p = 1\frac{2}{3}$

Bonus Box: Write five numbers that have ten digits each so that each number has the digit 5 in the hundredths place, and the sum of the digits is 66.

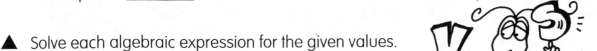

Name _____

▲ Multiply and divide. Simplify to lowest terms.

1.
$$1 \frac{3}{4} \div 3 \frac{1}{2} =$$

2.
$$5 \frac{5}{6} \times \frac{3}{10} =$$

3.
$$4 \frac{4}{5} \div 1 \frac{1}{15} =$$

4.
$$2 \frac{4}{7} \times 2 \frac{3}{9} =$$

5.
$$\frac{13}{16} \times 2 \frac{2}{3} =$$

6.
$$1 \frac{1}{2} \div 2 \frac{2}{11} =$$

▲ Draw tree diagrams to illustrate the possible combinations of snack and beverage choices.

Choose one beverage: Choose one snack:

    hot chocolate   pie
    pop   cake
    fruit juice   cookies
    water   fruit

What is the probability of having . . .

1. hot chocolate and pie? _____

2. fruit juice or pop with cookies? _____

3. cake? _____

4. water? _____

5. water and pie, cake, or cookies? _____

6. hot chocolate or fruit juice with cookies, cake, or fruit? _____

▲ Solve each algebraic expression for the given values.

1. $2.6p = 0.104$

      $p =$ _____

2. $.01 - r = .0036$

      $r =$ _____

3. $\frac{1}{2}g = \frac{1}{6}$

      $g =$ _____

Bonus Box: Write five fractions equivalent to $\frac{2}{3}$.

Name _____

▲ Solve. Simplify to lowest terms.

1. $7\dfrac{1}{5} \div 1\dfrac{1}{5} =$

2. $3\dfrac{1}{3} - 2\dfrac{2}{3} =$

3. $3\dfrac{3}{4} \times 1\dfrac{1}{5} =$

4. $2\dfrac{3}{4} + 4\dfrac{3}{4} =$

5. $9\dfrac{1}{5} - 2\dfrac{3}{5} =$

6. $2\dfrac{1}{10} \div 2\dfrac{4}{5} =$

▲ Solve for each letter.

1. $a = (b - t) \times a \div t$
$a \div t = 3$
$t + t + t = a$
$t < 3$
$3 < a < 8$

$a =$ _____ $b =$ _____ $t =$ _____

2. $s \div (p - r) - (m \times c) = c$
$c + c = m$
$m + m = p$
$1 + r = p$
$p + c = s$
$3 c = 6$

$c =$ _____ $m =$ _____ $p =$ _____ $r =$ _____ $s =$ _____

▲ Refer to the stem-and-leaf plot to answer the questions.

Numbers

7	3	3	5	6	7	7	9
6	2	4	5	5	6	8	9	9
5	0	1	2	2	5	7		
4	0	1	1	1	5	8		

1. What is the range? _____

2. Which number occurred most often? _____

3. What numbers are shown in the fourth leaf? _____

4. What is the mode? _____

5. What is the median? _____

Bonus Box: Write five problems with an answer of 2.14.

Answer Key

Mixed Skills in Math

Grades 5–6

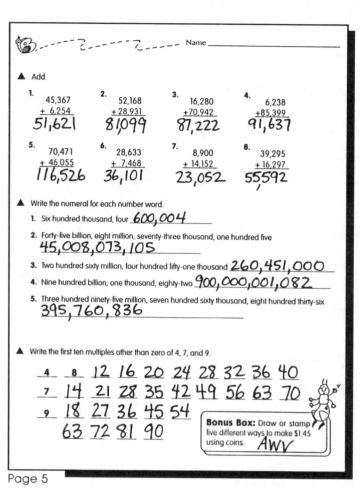

▲ Add.

1.	2.	3.	4.
45,367 + 6,254 = **51,621**	52,168 + 28,931 = **81,099**	16,280 + 70,942 = **87,222**	6,238 + 85,399 = **91,637**

5.	6.	7.	8.
70,471 + 46,055 = **116,526**	28,633 + 7,468 = **36,101**	8,900 + 14,152 = **23,052**	39,295 + 16,297 = **55,592**

▲ Write the numeral for each number word.

1. Six hundred thousand, four **600,004**

2. Forty-five billion, eight million, seventy-three thousand, one hundred five **45,008,073,105**

3. Two hundred sixty million, four hundred fifty-one thousand **260,451,000**

4. Nine hundred billion, one thousand, eighty-two **900,000,001,082**

5. Three hundred ninety-five million, seven hundred sixty thousand, eight hundred thirty-six **395,760,836**

▲ Write the first ten multiples other than zero of 4, 7, and 9.

4   8   12 16 20 24 28 32 36 40
7   14 21 28 35 42 49 56 63 70
9   18 27 36 45 54 63 72 81 90

Bonus Box: Draw or stamp five different ways to make $1.45 using coins. **AWV**

Page 5

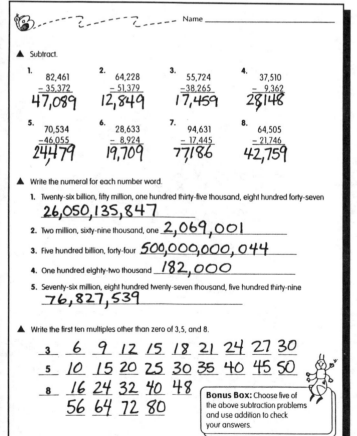

▲ Subtract.

1.	2.	3.	4.
82,461 − 35,372 = **47,089**	64,228 − 51,379 = **12,849**	55,724 − 38,265 = **17,459**	37,510 − 9,362 = **28,148**

5.	6.	7.	8.
70,534 − 46,055 = **24,479**	28,633 − 8,924 = **19,709**	94,631 − 17,445 = **77,186**	64,505 − 21,746 = **42,759**

▲ Write the numeral for each number word.

1. Twenty-six billion, fifty million, one hundred thirty-five thousand, eight hundred forty-seven **26,050,135,847**

2. Two million, sixty-nine thousand, one **2,069,001**

3. Five hundred billion, forty-four **500,000,000,044**

4. One hundred eighty-two thousand **182,000**

5. Seventy-six million, eight hundred twenty-seven thousand, five hundred thirty-nine **76,827,539**

▲ Write the first ten multiples other than zero of 3, 5, and 8.

3   6   9   12 15 18 21 24 27 30
5   10 15 20 25 30 35 40 45 50
8   16 24 32 40 48 56 64 72 80

Bonus Box: Choose five of the above subtraction problems and use addition to check your answers.

Page 6

104

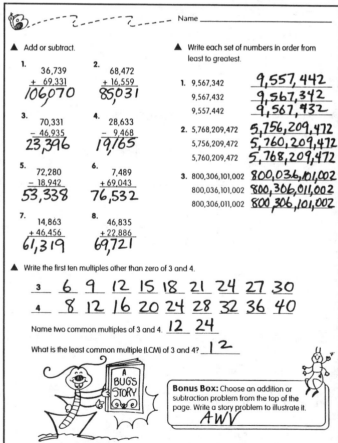

▲ Add or subtract.

1.	2.
36,739 + 69,331 = **106,070**	68,472 + 16,559 = **85,031**

3.	4.
70,331 − 46,935 = **23,396**	28,633 − 9,468 = **19,165**

5.	6.
72,280 − 18,942 = **53,338**	7,489 + 69,043 = **76,532**

7.	8.
14,863 + 46,456 = **61,319**	46,835 + 22,886 = **69,721**

▲ Write each set of numbers in order from least to greatest.

1.
9,567,342
9,567,432
9,557,442

9,557,442
9,567,342
9,567,432

2.
5,768,209,472
5,756,209,472
5,760,209,472

5,756,209,472
5,760,209,472
5,768,209,472

3.
800,306,101,002
800,036,101,002
800,306,011,002

800,036,101,002
800,306,011,002
800,306,101,002

▲ Write the first ten multiples other than zero of 3 and 4.

3   6   9   12 15 18 21 24 27 30
4   8   12 16 20 24 28 32 36 40

Name two common multiples of 3 and 4. **12   24**

What is the least common multiple (LCM) of 3 and 4? **12**

Bonus Box: Choose an addition or subtraction problem from the top of the page. Write a story problem to illustrate it. **AWV**

Page 7

© Carson-Dellosa   IF87123 • Mixed Skills in Math 5-6

Page 8

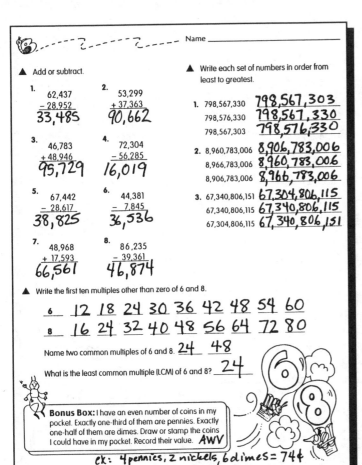

Name _____

▲ Add or subtract.

1. 62,437 − 28,952 = **33,485**
2. 53,299 + 37,363 = **90,662**
3. 46,783 + 48,946 = **95,729**
4. 72,304 − 56,285 = **16,019**
5. 67,442 − 28,617 = **38,825**
6. 44,381 − 7,845 = **36,536**
7. 48,968 + 17,593 = **66,561**
8. 86,235 − 39,361 = **46,874**

▲ Write each set of numbers in order from least to greatest.

1. 798,567,330 / 798,576,330 / 798,567,303 → **798,567,303 / 798,567,330 / 798,576,330**
2. 8,960,783,006 / 8,966,783,006 / 8,906,783,006 → **8,906,783,006 / 8,960,783,006 / 8,966,783,006**
3. 67,340,806,151 / 67,340,806,115 / 67,304,806,115 → **67,304,806,115 / 67,340,806,115 / 67,340,806,151**

▲ Write the first ten multiples other than zero of 6 and 8.

6   **12 18 24 30 36 42 48 54 60**
8   **16 24 32 40 48 56 64 72 80**

Name two common multiples of 6 and 8. **24   48**

What is the least common multiple (LCM) of 6 and 8? **24**

Bonus Box: I have an even number of coins in my pocket. Exactly one-third of them are pennies. Exactly one-half of them are dimes. Draw or stamp the coins I could have in my pocket. Record their value. **AWV**

ex: 4 pennies, 2 nickels, 6 dimes = 74¢

Page 8

Page 9

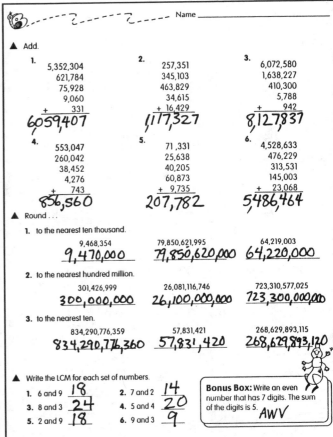

Name _____

▲ Add.

1.
```
  5,352,304
    621,784
     75,928
      9,060
  +     331
  6,059,407
```
2.
```
    257,351
    345,103
    463,829
     34,615
  + 16,429
  1,117,327
```
3.
```
  6,072,580
  1,638,227
    410,300
      5,788
  +    942
  8,127,837
```
4.
```
    553,047
    260,042
     38,452
      4,276
  +    743
    856,560
```
5.
```
     71,331
     25,638
     40,205
     60,873
  +  9,735
    207,782
```
6.
```
  4,528,633
    476,229
    313,531
    145,003
  + 23,068
  5,486,464
```

▲ Round . . .

1. to the nearest ten thousand.
   9,468,354 → **9,470,000**   79,850,621,995 → **79,850,620,000**   64,219,003 → **64,220,000**

2. to the nearest hundred million.
   301,426,999 → **300,000,000**   26,081,116,746 → **26,100,000,000**   723,310,577,025 → **723,300,000,000**

3. to the nearest ten.
   834,290,776,359 → **834,290,776,360**   57,831,421 → **57,831,420**   268,629,893,115 → **268,629,893,120**

▲ Write the LCM for each set of numbers.

1. 6 and 9   **18**
2. 7 and 2   **14**
3. 8 and 3   **24**
4. 5 and 4   **20**
5. 2 and 9   **18**
6. 9 and 3   **9**

Bonus Box: Write an even number that has 7 digits. The sum of the digits is 5. **AWV**

Page 9

Page 10

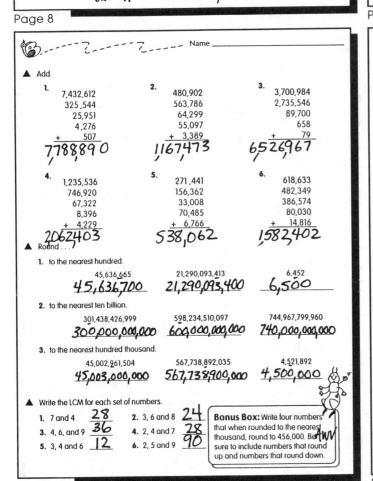

Name _____

▲ Add.

1.
```
  7,432,612
    325,544
     25,951
      4,276
  +    507
  7,788,890
```
2.
```
    480,902
    563,786
     64,299
     55,097
  +  3,389
  1,167,473
```
3.
```
  3,700,984
  2,735,546
     89,700
        658
  +     79
  6,526,967
```
4.
```
  1,235,536
    746,920
     67,322
      8,396
  +  4,229
  2,062,403
```
5.
```
    271,441
    156,362
     33,008
     70,485
  +  6,766
    538,062
```
6.
```
    618,633
    482,349
    386,574
     80,030
  + 14,816
  1,582,402
```

▲ Round . . .

1. to the nearest hundred.
   45,636,665 → **45,636,700**   21,290,093,413 → **21,290,093,400**   6,452 → **6,500**

2. to the nearest ten billion.
   301,438,426,999 → **300,000,000,000**   598,234,510,097 → **600,000,000,000**   744,967,799,960 → **740,000,000,000**

3. to the nearest hundred thousand.
   45,002,261,504 → **45,002,300,000**   567,738,892,035 → **567,738,900,000**   4,521,892 → **4,500,000**

▲ Write the LCM for each set of numbers.

1. 7 and 4   **28**
2. 3, 6 and 8   **24**
3. 4, 6, and 9   **36**
4. 2, 4 and 7   **28**
5. 3, 4 and 6   **12**
6. 2, 5 and 9   **90**

Bonus Box: Write four numbers that when rounded to the nearest thousand, round to 456,000. Be sure to include numbers that round up and numbers that round down. **AWV**

Page 10

Page 11

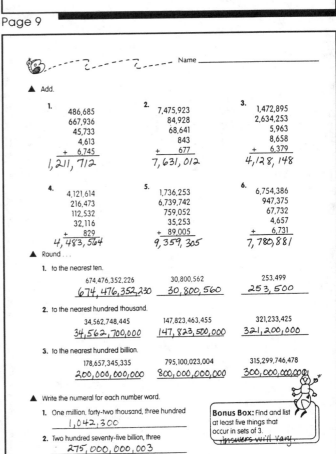

Name _____

▲ Add.

1.
```
    486,685
    667,936
     45,733
      4,613
  +  6,745
  1,211,712
```
2.
```
  7,475,923
     84,928
     68,641
        843
  +    677
  7,631,012
```
3.
```
  1,472,895
  2,634,253
      5,963
      8,658
  +  6,379
  4,128,148
```
4.
```
  4,121,614
    216,473
    112,532
     32,116
  +    829
  4,483,564
```
5.
```
  1,736,253
  6,739,742
    759,052
     35,253
  + 89,005
  9,359,305
```
6.
```
  6,754,386
    947,375
     67,732
      4,657
  +  6,731
  7,780,881
```

▲ Round . . .

1. to the nearest ten.
   674,476,352,226 → **674,476,352,230**   30,800,562 → **30,800,560**   253,499 → **253,500**

2. to the nearest hundred thousand.
   34,562,748,445 → **34,562,700,000**   147,823,463,455 → **147,823,500,000**   321,233,425 → **321,200,000**

3. to the nearest hundred billion.
   178,657,345,335 → **200,000,000,000**   795,100,023,004 → **800,000,000,000**   315,299,746,478 → **300,000,000,000**

▲ Write the numeral for each number word.

1. One million, forty-two thousand, three hundred
   1,042,300

2. Two hundred seventy-five billion, three
   275,000,000,003

Bonus Box: Find and list at least five things that occur in sets of 3. Answers will vary.

Page 11

105

Page 12

▲ Subtract.

1.	2.	3.	4.
452,567 − 154,859 **297,708**	532,112 − 254,264 **277,848**	724,324 − 152,578 **571,746**	246,132 − 58,394 **187,738**

5.	6.	7.	8.
703,523 − 612,408 **91,115**	923,811 − 74,426 **849,385**	823,645 − 541,773 **281,872**	432,363 − 153,856 **278,507**

▲ Use front-end estimation to estimate each sum.
The first one is done for you.

1.	2.
463 **500** + 218 **+200** **700**	290 **300** + 472 **500** **800**

▲ Write each set of numbers in order from least to greatest.

1. 465,543,376   **465453367**
465,453,367   **465543367**
465,543,367   **465543376**

3.	4.
182 **200** + 563 **600** **800**	54,285 **50,000** + 32,687 **30,000** **80,000**

2. 790,574,400,503   **709547400503**
790,547,400,503   **790,547,400,503**
709,547,400,503   **790,574,400,503**

5.	6.
4,621 **5,000** + 1,532 **2,000** **7,000**	34,625 **30,000** + 37,543 **40,000** **70,000**

3. 20,593,557,408   **20,593,557,408**
20,593,575,408   **20,593,557,480**
20,593,557,480   **20,593,575,408**

7.	8.
3,674 **4,000** + 4,463 **4,000** **8,000**	2,754 **3,000** + 4,343 **4,000** **7,000**

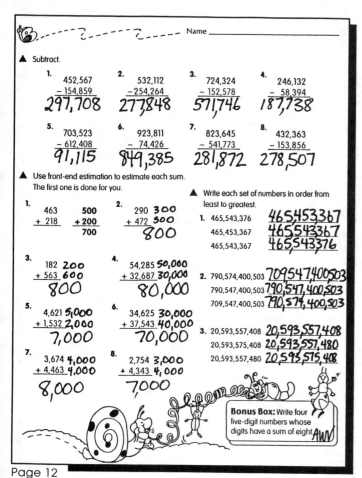

Bonus Box: Write four five-digit numbers whose digits have a sum of eight. AWV

Page 12

Page 13

▲ Subtract.

1.	2.	3.	4.
35,452,567 − 6,744,859 **28,707,708**	11,253,645 − 6,745,365 **4,508,280**	62,703,523 − 61,367,863 **1,335,660**	73,623,811 − 72,896,424 **727,387**

5.	6.	7.	8.
90,464,766 − 1,526,899 **88,937,867**	37,564,366 − 19,578,897 **17,985,469**	4,532,067 − 2,541,773 **1,990,294**	93,432,363 − 64,674,274 **28,758,089**

▲ Use front-end estimation to estimate each sum. The first one is done for you.

1.	2.	3.
743 **700** + 632 **+600** **1,300**	583,639 **600,000** +162,265 **200,000** **800,000**	3,673 **4,000** + 2,415 **2,000** **6,000**

4.	5.	6.
314,526 **300,000** + 415,515 **400,000** **700,000**	3,425 **3,000** + 2,397 **2,000** **5,000**	45,632 **50000** + 18,536 **20,000** **70,000**

7.	8.	9.
7,221 **7,000** + 1,186 **1,000** **8,000**	473 **500** + 365 **400** **900**	8,345 **8,000** + 1,623 **2,000** **10,000**

▲ Write the LCM for each set of numbers.

1. 5 and 9   **45**
2. 2 and 3   **6**
3. 6 and 9   **18**
4. 3, 5 and 6   **30**
5. 3, 6 and 15   **30**
6. 4, 6 and 7   **84**
7. 4, 6 and 10   **60**
8. 2, 3 and 12   **12**

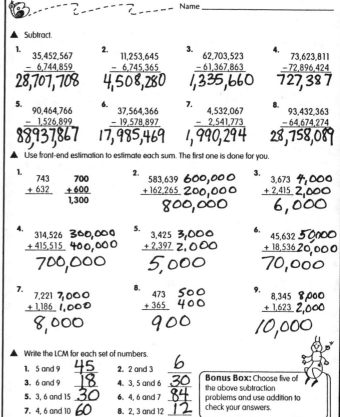

Bonus Box: Choose five of the above subtraction problems and use addition to check your answers.

Page 13

Page 14

▲ Subtract.

1.	2.	3.	4.
600,000 − 44,859 **555,141**	10,000,000 − 5,210,987 **4,789,013**	900,000 − 526,899 **373,101**	70,000,000 − 57,364,325 **12,635,675**

5.	6.	7.	8.
20,000,000 − 1,369,853 **18,630,147**	50,000,000 − 32,821,424 **17,178,576**	40,000,000 − 22,541,336 **17,458,664**	9,000,000 − 2,674,274 **6,325,726**

▲ Multiply.

1.	2.	3.	4.	5.
8 × 4 **32**	6 × 7 **42**	5 × 9 **45**	9 × 8 **72**	2 × 7 **14**

6.	7.	8.	9.	10.
7 × 7 **49**	9 × 6 **54**	4 × 7 **28**	8 × 8 **64**	8 × 3 **24**

▲ Round . . . .

1. to the nearest ten million.

45,839,208,211   **45,840,000,000**   672,899,905   **670,000,000**   5,398,210,647   **5,400,000,000**

2. to the nearest hundred.

56,382,019   **56,382,000**   674,291,108,223   **674,291,108,200**   674,892   **674,900**

3. to the nearest thousand.

633,298,987,028   **633,298,987,000**   62,165,119,624   **62,165,120,000**

Bonus Box: Choose one subtraction and two multiplication problems from this page. Write a story problem for each. AWV

Page 14

106

Page 15

▲ Subtract.

1.	2.
70,030 − 54,269 **15,761**	80,020,000 − 31,210,658 **48,809,342**

▲ Multiply.

1. 6 × 8 = **48**
2. 5 × 7 = **35**
3. 6 × 6 = **36**
4. 9 × 8 = **72**
5. 9 × 3 = **27**
6. 3 × 6 = **18**
7. 7 × 8 = **56**
8. 5 × 8 = **40**
9. 7 × 9 = **63**
10. 2 × 8 = **16**
11. 7 × 6 = **42**
12. 9 × 4 = **36**

3.	4.
2,001,100 − 1,524,838 **476,262**	400,000 − 361,865 **38,135**

5.	6.
90,005,000 − 41,731,852 **48,273,148**	1,026,000 − 215,469 **810,531**

7.	8.
600,010 − 422,541 **177,469**	30,600,400 − 18,654,417 **11,945,983**

▲ Use front-end estimation to estimate each sum or difference.

1.	2.
4,729 **5000** + 1,099 **1000** **6,000**	883,649 **900,000** − 462,265 **500,000** **400,000**

3.	4.
526,362 **500,000** + 215,875 **200,000** **700,000**	28,425 **30,000** + 50,397 **50,000** **80,000**

5.	6.
845,632 **800,000** − 186,536 **200,000** **600,000**	5,673 **6,000** − 2,415 **2,000** **4,000**

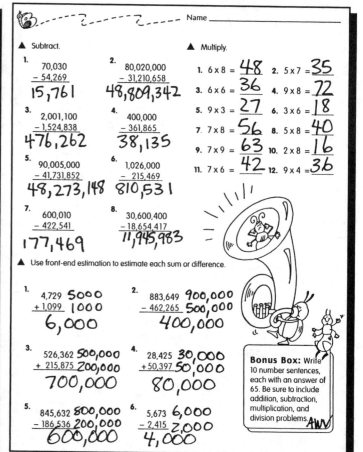

Bonus Box: Write 10 number sentences, each with an answer of 65. Be sure to include addition, subtraction, multiplication, and division problems. AWV

Page 15

Page 16

Name _____

▲ Subtract.

1. 45,890,000
− 21,564,269
24,325,731

2. 17,300,542
− 10,658,839
6,641,703

3. 893,001
− 396,273
496,728

4. 9,000,120
− 728,203
8,271,917

5. 80,000,000
− 61,173,862
18,826,138

6. 98,500,300
− 21,785,469
76,714,831

7. 320,001
− 102,546
217,455

8. 60,004,100
− 14,085,307
45,918,793

▲ Record the perimeter.

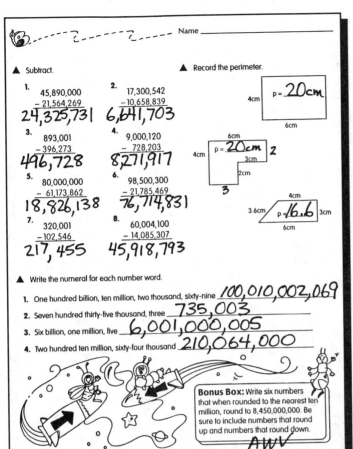

p = **20cm** (4cm × 6cm)

p = **20cm** (6cm, 4cm, 3cm, 2cm)

p = **16.6** (4cm, 3.6cm, 3cm, 6cm)

▲ Write the numeral for each number word.

1. One hundred billion, ten million, two thousand, sixty-nine **100,010,002,069**
2. Seven hundred thirty-five thousand, three **735,003**
3. Six billion, one million, five **6,001,000,005**
4. Two hundred ten million, sixty-four thousand **210,064,000**

Bonus Box: Write six numbers that when rounded to the nearest ten million, round to 8,450,000,000. Be sure to include numbers that round up and numbers that round down. **AWV**

Page 17

Name _____

▲ On lined paper, arrange in columns and add. Write the sums here.

1. 242 + 67 + 85 + 463 + 689 + 58 + 147 + 38 = **1,789**
2. 845 + 1,603 + 54 + 286 + 3,661 + 598 + 2,286 = **9,333**
3. 861 + 99 + 38 + 5,484 + 27 + 6,310 + 77 + 184 = **13,080**
4. 2,809 + 465 + 94 + 56,893 + 811 + 51,382 + 38 = **112,492**
5. 273 + 574 + 29 + 36 + 6,382 + 43 + 7,386 + 48 + 82 = **14,853**

▲ Label the Venn diagram.

Multiples of 3   Even Numbers

9, 15, 21, 3 | 12, 18, 6 | 8, 4, 20, 10, 14

▲ Multiply.

1. 6 × 6 = **36**
2. 8 × 5 = **40**
3. 9 × 4 = **36**
4. 3 × 7 = **21**
5. 5 × 9 = **45**
6. 4 × 7 = **28**
7. 6 × 9 = **54**
8. 7 × 8 = **56**
9. 8 × 9 = **72**
10. 7 × 6 = **42**

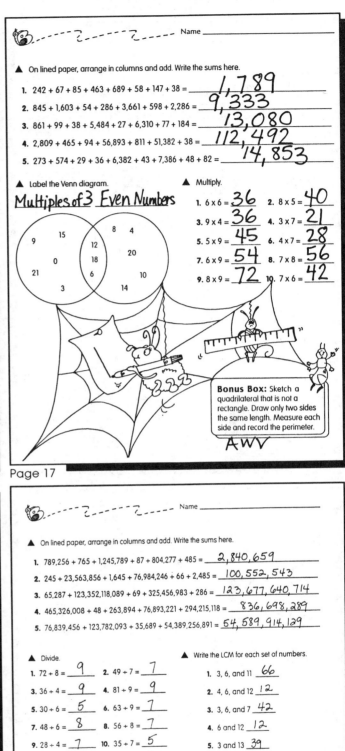

Bonus Box: Sketch a quadrilateral that is not a rectangle. Draw only two sides the same length. Measure each side and record the perimeter. **AWV**

Page 18

Name _____

▲ On lined paper, arrange in columns and add. Write the sums here.

1. 45,678 + 869 + 5,629 + 8,311 + 632 + 28 + 746 = **61,893**
2. 667 + 3,845 + 62,327 + 162 + 45,362 + 3,522 + 73 = **115,958**
3. 14,626 + 734 + 6,823 + 61,415 + 774 + 11,182 + 248 = **95,802**
4. 6,272 + 118 + 926 + 21,721 + 62,006 + 704 + 2,781 = **94,528**
5. 91 + 728 + 7,283 + 511 + 79 + 2,617 + 28,837 + 821 = **40,967**

▲ Divide.

1. 24 ÷ 4 = **6**
2. 36 ÷ 6 = **6**
3. 42 ÷ 7 = **6**
4. 45 ÷ 5 = **9**
5. 48 ÷ 8 = **6**
6. 63 ÷ 9 = **7**
7. 49 ÷ 7 = **7**
8. 72 ÷ 8 = **9**
9. 27 ÷ 3 = **9**
10. 28 ÷ 4 = **7**
11. 25 ÷ 5 = **5**
12. 35 ÷ 7 = **5**

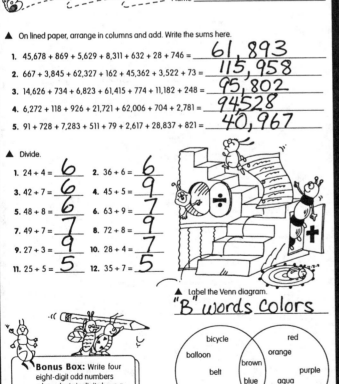

▲ Label the Venn diagram.

"B" words   Colors

bicycle, balloon, belt, bear, battery | brown, blue | red, orange, purple, aqua, maroon

Bonus Box: Write four eight-digit odd numbers whose last six digits have a sum of ten. **AWV**

Page 19

Name _____

▲ On lined paper, arrange in columns and add. Write the sums here.

1. 789,256 + 765 + 1,245,789 + 87 + 804,277 + 485 = **2,840,659**
2. 245 + 23,563,856 + 1,645 + 76,984,246 + 66 + 2,485 = **100,552,543**
3. 65,287 + 123,352,118,089 + 69 + 325,456,983 + 286 = **123,677,640,714**
4. 465,326,008 + 48 + 263,894 + 76,893,221 + 294,215,118 = **836,698,289**
5. 76,839,456 + 123,782,093 + 35,689 + 54,389,256,891 = **54,589,914,129**

▲ Divide.

1. 72 ÷ 8 = **9**
2. 49 ÷ 7 = **7**
3. 36 ÷ 4 = **9**
4. 81 ÷ 9 = **9**
5. 30 ÷ 6 = **5**
6. 63 ÷ 9 = **7**
7. 48 ÷ 6 = **8**
8. 56 ÷ 8 = **7**
9. 28 ÷ 4 = **7**
10. 35 ÷ 7 = **5**
11. 56 ÷ 7 = **8**
12. 72 ÷ 9 = **8**

▲ Write the LCM for each set of numbers.

1. 3, 6, and 11 **66**
2. 4, 6, and 12 **12**
3. 3, 6, and 7 **42**
4. 6 and 12 **12**
5. 3 and 13 **39**
6. 6 and 9 **18**

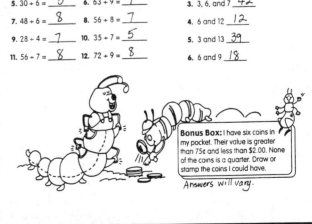

Bonus Box: I have six coins in my pocket. Their value is greater than 75¢ and less than $2.00. None of the coins is a quarter. Draw or stamp the coins I could have. **Answers will vary.**

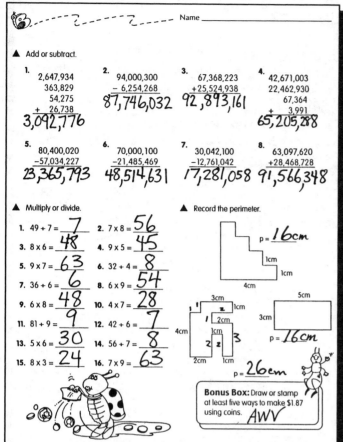

Page 20

▲ Add or subtract.

1.
2,647,934
363,829
54,275
+ 26,738
3,092,776

2.
94,000,300
− 6,254,268
87,746,032

3.
67,368,223
+25,524,938
92,893,161

4.
42,671,003
22,462,930
67,364
+ 3,991
65,205,288

5.
80,400,020
−57,034,227
23,365,793

6.
70,000,100
−21,485,469
48,514,631

7.
30,042,100
−12,761,042
17,281,058

8.
63,097,620
+28,468,728
91,566,348

▲ Multiply or divide.

1. 49 + 7 = **7**
2. 7 x 8 = **56**
3. 8 x 6 = **48**
4. 9 x 5 = **45**
5. 9 x 7 = **63**
6. 32 + 4 = **8**
7. 36 + 6 = **6**
8. 6 x 9 = **54**
9. 6 x 8 = **48**
10. 4 x 7 = **28**
11. 81 + 9 = **9**
12. 42 + 6 = **7**
13. 5 x 6 = **30**
14. 56 + 7 = **8**
15. 8 x 3 = **24**
16. 7 x 9 = **63**

▲ Record the perimeter.

p = **16cm**

1cm
1cm
4cm

3cm
1cm
2cm
4cm
2cm 1cm
2cm 1cm

5cm
3cm
p = **16cm**

p = **26cm**

Bonus Box: Draw or stamp at least five ways to make $1.87 using coins. **AWV**

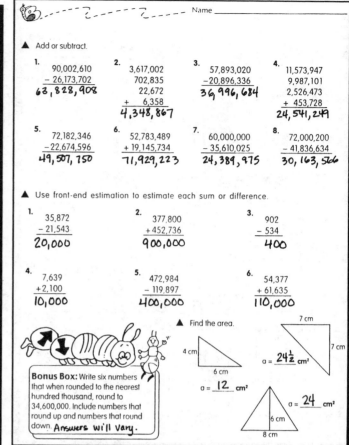

Page 21

▲ Add or subtract.

1.
90,002,610
− 26,173,702
63,828,908

2.
3,617,002
702,835
22,672
+ 6,358
4,348,867

3.
57,893,020
−20,896,336
36,996,684

4.
11,573,947
9,987,101
2,526,473
+ 453,728
24,541,249

5.
72,182,346
−22,674,596
49,507,750

6.
52,783,489
+ 19,145,734
71,929,223

7.
60,000,000
− 35,610,025
24,389,975

8.
72,000,200
− 41,836,634
30,163,566

▲ Use front-end estimation to estimate each sum or difference.

1.
35,872
− 21,543
20,000

2.
377,800
+452,736
900,000

3.
902
− 534
400

4.
7,639
+2,100
10,000

5.
472,984
− 119,897
400,000

6.
54,377
+ 61,635
110,000

Bonus Box: Write six numbers that when rounded to the nearest hundred thousand, round to 34,600,000. Include numbers that round up and numbers that round down. **Answers will vary.**

▲ Find the area.

7 cm
4 cm
6 cm
a = **12** cm²

7 cm
a = **24½** cm²

6 cm
8 cm
a = **24** cm²

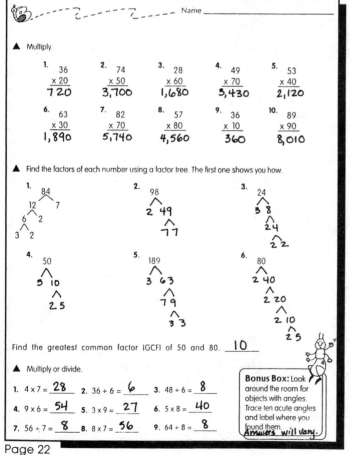

Page 22

▲ Multiply.

1.
36
x 20
720

2.
74
x 50
3,700

3.
28
x 60
1,680

4.
49
x 70
3,430

5.
53
x 40
2,120

6.
63
x 30
1,890

7.
82
x 70
5,740

8.
57
x 80
4,560

9.
36
x 10
360

10.
89
x 90
8,010

▲ Find the factors of each number using a factor tree. The first one shows you how.

1.
84
12 7
6 2
3 2

2.
98
2 49
7 7

3.
24
3 8
2 4
2 2

4.
50
5 10
2 5

5.
189
3 63
7 9
3 3

6.
80
2 40
2 20
2 10
2 5

Find the greatest common factor (GCF) of 50 and 80. **10**

▲ Multiply or divide.

1. 4 x 7 = **28**
2. 36 + 6 = **6**
3. 48 + 6 = **8**
4. 9 x 6 = **54**
5. 3 x 9 = **27**
6. 5 x 8 = **40**
7. 56 + 7 = **8**
8. 8 x 7 = **56**
9. 64 + 8 = **8**

Bonus Box: Look around the room for objects with angles. Trace ten acute angles and label where you found them. **Answers will vary.**

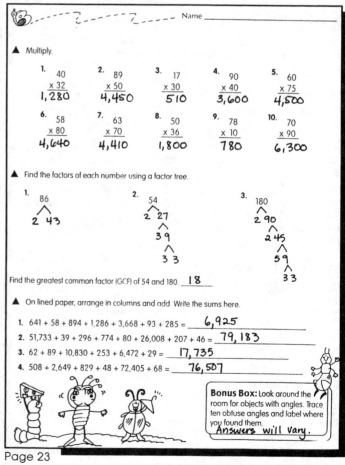

Page 23

▲ Multiply.

1.
40
x 32
1,280

2.
89
x 50
4,450

3.
17
x 30
510

4.
90
x 40
3,600

5.
60
x 75
4,500

6.
58
x 80
4,640

7.
63
x 70
4,410

8.
50
x 36
1,800

9.
78
x 10
780

10.
70
x 90
6,300

▲ Find the factors of each number using a factor tree.

1.
86
2 43

2.
54
2 27
3 9
3 3

3.
180
2 90
2 45
5 9
3 3

Find the greatest common factor (GCF) of 54 and 180. **18**

▲ On lined paper, arrange in columns and add. Write the sums here.

1. 641 + 58 + 894 + 1,286 + 3,668 + 93 + 285 = **6,925**
2. 51,733 + 39 + 296 + 774 + 80 + 26,008 + 207 + 46 = **79,183**
3. 62 + 89 + 10,830 + 253 + 6,472 + 29 = **17,735**
4. 508 + 2,649 + 829 + 48 + 72,405 + 68 = **76,507**

Bonus Box: Look around the room for objects with angles. Trace ten obtuse angles and label where you found them. **Answers will vary.**

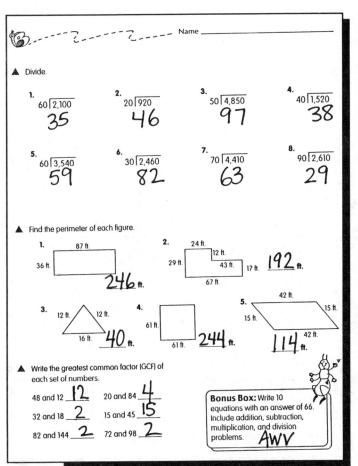

Page 24

▲ Divide.

1. $60\overline{)2{,}100}$ = 35
2. $20\overline{)920}$ = 46
3. $50\overline{)4{,}850}$ = 97
4. $40\overline{)1{,}520}$ = 38
5. $60\overline{)3{,}540}$ = 59
6. $30\overline{)2{,}460}$ = 82
7. $70\overline{)4{,}410}$ = 63
8. $90\overline{)2{,}610}$ = 29

▲ Find the perimeter of each figure.

1. 87 ft, 36 ft = 246 ft
2. 24 ft, 12 ft, 29 ft, 43 ft, 67 ft, 17 ft = 192 ft
3. 12 ft, 12 ft, 16 ft = 40 ft
4. square 61 ft, 61 ft = 244 ft
5. 42 ft, 15 ft, 15 ft, 42 ft = 114 ft

▲ Write the greatest common factor (GCF) of each set of numbers.

48 and 12 = 12   20 and 84 = 4
32 and 18 = 2   15 and 45 = 15
82 and 144 = 2   72 and 98 = 2

Bonus Box: Write 10 equations with an answer of 66. Include addition, subtraction, multiplication, and division problems. AWV

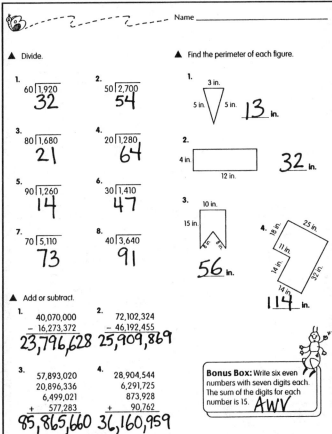

Page 25

▲ Divide.

1. $60\overline{)1{,}920}$ = 32
2. $50\overline{)2{,}700}$ = 54
3. $80\overline{)1{,}680}$ = 21
4. $20\overline{)1{,}280}$ = 64
5. $90\overline{)1{,}260}$ = 14
6. $30\overline{)1{,}410}$ = 47
7. $70\overline{)5{,}110}$ = 73
8. $40\overline{)3{,}640}$ = 91

▲ Add or subtract.

1.
```
  40,070,000
- 16,273,372
```
23,796,628

2.
```
  72,102,324
- 46,192,455
```
25,909,869

3.
```
  57,893,020
  20,896,336
   6,499,021
+    577,283
```
85,865,660

4.
```
  28,904,544
   6,291,725
     873,928
+     90,762
```
36,160,959

▲ Find the perimeter of each figure.

1. 3 in, 5 in, 5 in = 13 in
2. 4 in, 12 in = 32 in
3. 10 in, 15 in = 56 in
4. 18 in, 25 in, 11 in, 14 in, 32 in, 14 in = 114 in

Bonus Box: Write six even numbers with seven digits each. The sum of the digits for each number is 15. AWV

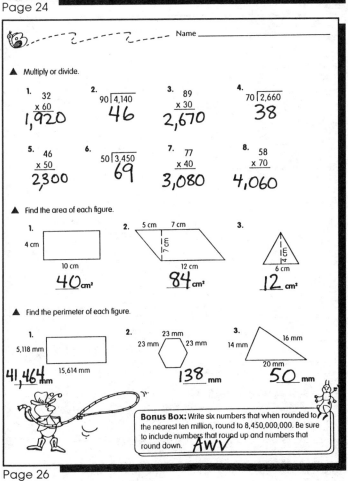

Page 26

▲ Multiply or divide.

1.
```
   32
 × 60
```
1,920

2. $90\overline{)4{,}140}$ = 46

3.
```
   89
 × 30
```
2,670

4. $70\overline{)2{,}660}$ = 38

5.
```
   46
 × 50
```
2,300

6. $50\overline{)3{,}450}$ = 69

7.
```
   77
 × 40
```
3,080

8.
```
   58
 × 70
```
4,060

▲ Find the area of each figure.

1. 4 cm, 10 cm = 40 cm²
2. 5 cm, 7 cm, 7 cm, 12 cm = 84 cm²
3. 6 cm = 12 cm²

▲ Find the perimeter of each figure.

1. 5,118 mm, 15,614 mm = 41,464 mm
2. 23 mm, 23 mm, 23 mm = 138 mm
3. 14 mm, 16 mm, 20 mm = 50 mm

Bonus Box: Write six numbers that when rounded to the nearest ten million, round to 8,450,000,000. Be sure to include numbers that round up and numbers that round down. AWV

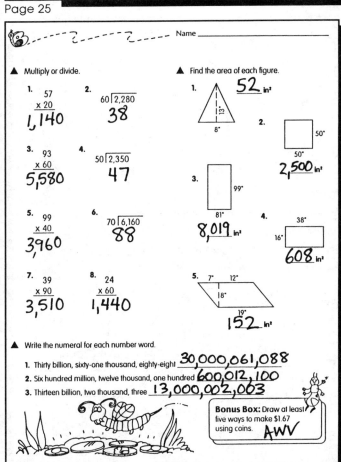

Page 27

▲ Multiply or divide.

1.
```
   57
 × 20
```
1,140

2. $60\overline{)2{,}280}$ = 38

3.
```
   93
 × 60
```
5,580

4. $50\overline{)2{,}350}$ = 47

5.
```
   99
 × 40
```
3,960

6. $70\overline{)6{,}160}$ = 88

7.
```
   39
 × 90
```
3,510

8.
```
   24
 × 60
```
1,440

▲ Find the area of each figure.

1. 13, 8 = 52 in²
2. 50, 50 = 2,500 in²
3. 99, 81 = 8,019 in²
4. 38, 16 = 608 in²
5. 7, 12, 18, 19 = 152 in²

▲ Write the numeral for each number word.

1. Thirty billion, sixty-one thousand, eighty-eight = 30,000,061,088
2. Six hundred million, twelve thousand, one hundred = 600,012,100
3. Thirteen billion, two thousand, three = 13,000,002,003

Bonus Box: Draw at least five ways to make $1.67 using coins. AWV

Page 28

▲ Multiply.

1. 52 × 13 = **676**
2. 21 × 68 = **1,428**
3. 13 × 23 = **299**
4. 43 × 22 = **946**
5. 14 × 12 = **168**
6. 31 × 39 = **1,209**
7. 72 × 14 = **1,008**
8. 33 × 31 = **1,023**

▲ Round . . .

1. to the nearest tenth.

526.78 → **526.8**   43,821.29 → **43,821.3**   5,246.81 → **5,246.8**

2. to the nearest hundredth.

25.252 → **25.25**   386.916 → **386.92**   44,643.426 → **44,643.43**

3. to the nearest thousandth.

28.9215 → **28.922**   567,543.2663 → **567,543.266**   8.3647 → **8.365**

Bonus Box: Look around the room for objects with angles. Make a graph to show how many right, obtuse and acute angles you find. Write two statements about your data. **AWV**

▲ Find the perimeter of each figure.

1. square 2,689cm × 2,689cm → **10,756 cm**
2. rhombus 65mm, 40mm → **210 mm**

Page 28

Page 29

▲ Multiply.

1. 26 × 41 = **1,066**
2. 53 × 62 = **3,286**
3. 42 × 74 = **3,108**
4. 65 × 51 = **3,315**
5. 83 × 43 = **3,569**
6. 62 × 64 = **3,968**
7. 41 × 58 = **2,378**
8. 80 × 26 = **2,080**

▲ Graph the following data about Yesenia's family vacation.

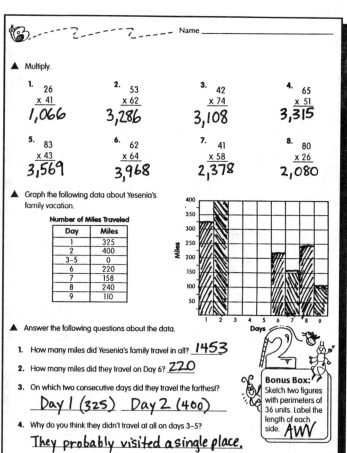

Number of Miles Traveled

Day	Miles
1	325
2	400
3–5	0
6	220
7	158
8	240
9	110

▲ Answer the following questions about the data.

1. How many miles did Yesenia's family travel in all? **1453**
2. How many miles did they travel on Day 6? **220**
3. On which two consecutive days did they travel the farthest? **Day 1 (325)   Day 2 (400)**
4. Why do you think they didn't travel at all on days 3–5?

They probably visited a single place.

Bonus Box: Sketch two figures with perimeters of 36 units. Label the length of each side. **AWV**

Page 29

Page 30

▲ Multiply.

1. 47 × 63 = **2,961**
2. 54 × 36 = **1,944**
3. 27 × 45 = **1,215**
4. 84 × 19 = **1,596**
5. 37 × 24 = **888**
6. 47 × 65 = **3,055**
7. 78 × 32 = **2,496**
8. 44 × 65 = **2,860**

▲ Write the numeral for each number word.

1. Three hundred five and twenty-five hundredths **305.25**
2. Eight and one hundred forty-two thousandths **8.142**
3. Two million, five and three hundred fifty-one thousandths **2,000,005.351**
4. Five thousand and six hundredths **5,000.06**

▲ Find the area of each figure.

1. parallelogram 3 cm, 15 cm, 10 cm, 18 cm → **180 cm²**
2. square 62 cm, 62 cm → **3,844 cm²**
3. rectangle 47 m, 65 m → **3,055 m²**

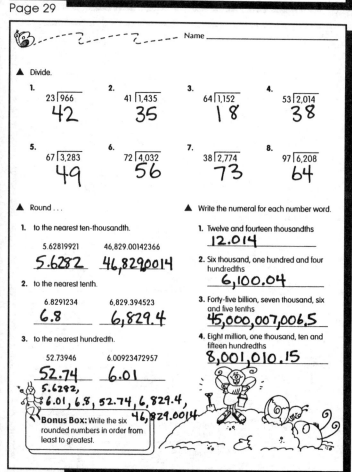

Bonus Box: Sketch two different rectangles with perimeters of 68 units. Label the length of each side. What is the area of each rectangle? Compare the areas and explain your answers. **AWV**

Page 30

Page 31

▲ Divide.

1. 23)966 = **42**
2. 41)1,435 = **35**
3. 64)1,152 = **18**
4. 53)2,014 = **38**
5. 67)3,283 = **49**
6. 72)4,032 = **56**
7. 38)2,774 = **73**
8. 97)6,208 = **64**

▲ Round . . .

1. to the nearest ten-thousandth.

5.62819921 → **5.6282**   46,829.00142366 → **46,829.0014**

2. to the nearest tenth.

6.8291234 → **6.8**   6,829.394523 → **6,829.4**

3. to the nearest hundredth.

52.73946 → **52.74**   6.00923472957 → **6.01**

▲ Write the numeral for each number word.

1. Twelve and fourteen thousandths **12.014**
2. Six thousand, one hundred and four hundredths **6,100.04**
3. Forty-five billion, seven thousand, six and five tenths **45,000,007,006.5**
4. Eight million, one thousand, ten and fifteen hundredths **8,001,010.15**

Bonus Box: Write the six rounded numbers in order from least to greatest.
5.6282, 6.01, 6.8, 52.74, 6,829.4, 46,829.0014

Page 31

Page 32

▲ Divide.

1. $45\overline{)1,035}$ **23**
2. $27\overline{)2,322}$ **86**
3. $53\overline{)2,173}$ **41**
4. $67\overline{)1,206}$ **18**

5. $32\overline{)3,104}$ **97**
6. $58\overline{)3,596}$ **62**
7. $76\overline{)4,028}$ **53**
8. $41\overline{)1,394}$ **34**

▲ Write each set of numbers in order from least to greatest.

1. 2,648.23145
   264.823145
   26,482.3145

   264.823145
   2,648.23145
   26,482.3145

2. 6.198002
   6.19002
   6.189002

   6.189002
   6.19002
   6.198002

3. 26.586102
   25.86102
   25.68102

   25.68102
   25.86102
   26.586102

▲ Identify the length of **X** in each figure.

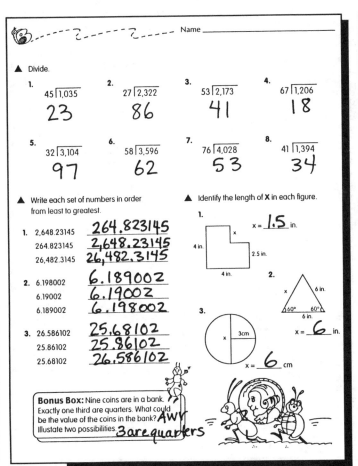

1. x = **1.5** in.
2. x = **6** in.
3. x = **6** cm

Bonus Box: Nine coins are in a bank. Exactly one third are quarters. What could be the value of the coins in the bank? Illustrate two possibilities. **AWV 3 are quarters**

Page 32

Page 33

▲ Divide.

1. $24\overline{)876}$ **36 R12**
2. $47\overline{)2,894}$ **61 R27**
3. $72\overline{)1,207}$ **16 R55**
4. $53\overline{)2,260}$ **42 R34**

5. $36\overline{)3,174}$ **88 R6**
6. $69\overline{)1,838}$ **26 R44**
7. $83\overline{)3,961}$ **47 R60**
8. $15\overline{)708}$ **47 R3**

▲ Write each set of numbers in order from least to greatest.

1. 4.675904
   46.75904
   4.657904

   4.657904
   4.675904
   46.75904

2. 0.53442
   0.53424
   05.3442

   0.53424
   0.53442
   05.3442

3. 367.38291
   36.738291
   36.378291

   36.378291
   36.738291
   367.38291

▲ Write the least common multiple (LCM) for each set of numbers.

1. 2 and 7 **14**
2. 4 and 10 **20**
3. 6 and 8 **24**
4. 5 and 3 **15**
5. 11 and 3 **33**
6. 10 and 6 **30**
7. 12 and 6 **12**
8. 5 and 2 **10**
9. 6 and 9 **18**

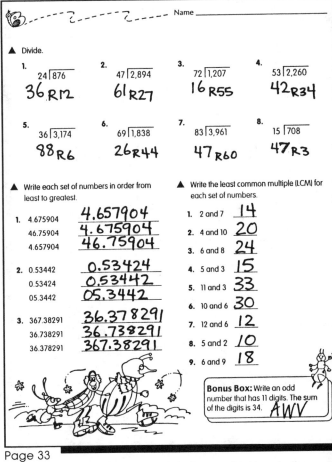

Bonus Box: Write an odd number that has 11 digits. The sum of the digits is 34. **AWV**

Page 33

Page 34

▲ Divide.

1. $34\overline{)409}$ **12 R1**
2. $57\overline{)4,663}$ **81 R46**
3. $12\overline{)1,168}$ **97 R4**
4. $22\overline{)865}$ **39 R7**

5. $72\overline{)1,797}$ **24 R69**
6. $41\overline{)3,214}$ **78 R16**
7. $99\overline{)5,612}$ **56 R68**
8. $67\overline{)3,340}$ **49 R57**

▲ Add.

1.
   58.864701
   7.152677
   + 9.38576
   75.403138

2.
   6,743.00921
   934.279488
   + 1,546.98032
   9,224.269018

3.
   158.53774
   45.627384
   + 5,821.27843
   6,025.443554

4.
   4,627.095054
   264.2723
   6.800989
   4898.168343

▲ Write the numeral for each number word.

1. Three billion, forty-four and six hundredths **3,000,000,044.06**
2. Four hundred sixty-eight thousandths **.468**
3. Three and two hundred five thousandths **3.205**

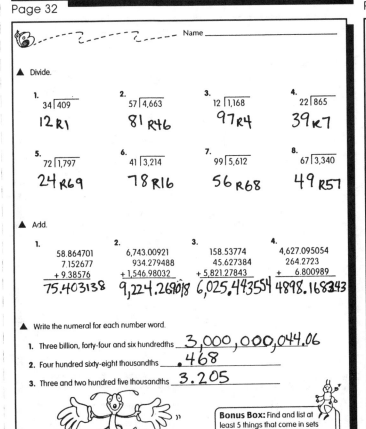

Bonus Box: Find and list at least 5 things that come in sets of two. **AWV**

Page 34

Page 35

▲ Multiply or divide.

1.
   52
   x 67
   3,484

2. $34\overline{)2,231}$ **65 R21**

3. $15\overline{)723}$ **48 R.3**

4.
   71
   x 29
   2,059

5. $48\overline{)1,694}$ **35 R.14**

6. $68\overline{)2,015}$ **29 R.43**

7.
   83
   x 59
   4,897

8.
   37
   x 63
   2,331

▲ Add.

1.
   463.900827
   54.82914
   + 2,473.241
   2,991.970967

2.
   7.920343
   3.22416
   + 63.786869
   74.931372

3.
   123.415266
   64.73786
   + 748.342756
   936.495882

4.
   5.487969
   43.65647
   + 2.6214658
   51.7659048

▲ On lined paper, arrange in columns and add. Write the sums here.

1. 3,786 + 23 + 657 + 85 + 7,543 + 283 + 972 = **13,349**
2. 78 + 354 + 62 + 4,536 + 3,270 + 84 + 28 + 99 + 31 = **8,542**
3. 5,600 + 243 + 694 + 6,453 + 89 + 39 + 64 + 57 = **13,239**

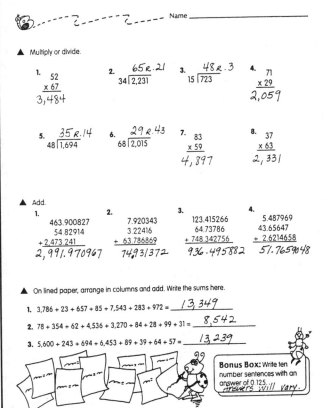

Bonus Box: Write ten number sentences with an answer of 0.125. **Answers will vary.**

Page 35

Page 36

▲ Multiply or divide.

1. $47\overline{)2,740}$ **58 R14**
2. $86\overline{)2,047}$ **23 R69**
3. $\begin{array}{r} 64 \\ \times 53 \\ \hline \end{array}$ **3,392**
4. $\begin{array}{r} 39 \\ \times 44 \\ \hline \end{array}$ **1,716**

5. $\begin{array}{r} 78 \\ \times 36 \\ \hline \end{array}$ **2,808**
6. $32\overline{)2,657}$ **83 R1**
7. $74\overline{)3,043}$ **41 R9**
8. $\begin{array}{r} 21 \\ \times 79 \\ \hline \end{array}$ **1,659**

▲ Subtract.

1. $\begin{array}{r} 632.52231 \\ -\ 56.32743 \\ \hline \end{array}$ **576.19488**
2. $\begin{array}{r} 54.622 \\ -\ 32.8653 \\ \hline \end{array}$ **21.7567**
3. $\begin{array}{r} 362.1106 \\ -\ 170.26153 \\ \hline \end{array}$ **191.84907**
4. $\begin{array}{r} 1.5672 \\ -\ 0.834267 \\ \hline \end{array}$ **.732933**

5. $\begin{array}{r} 6.8 \\ -\ 2.6437 \\ \hline \end{array}$ **4.1563**
6. $\begin{array}{r} 1,674.21 \\ -\ 547.446 \\ \hline \end{array}$ **1,126.764**

▲ Write the greatest common factor (GCF) of each set of numbers.

1. 64 and 120   **8**
2. 90 and 105   **15**
3. 42 and 70   **14**
4. 60 and 36   **12**
5. 126 and 84   **42**
6. 144 and 162   **18**

Bonus Box: Sketch five different polygons. Assign each side a length and give the perimeter for each figure. **AWV**

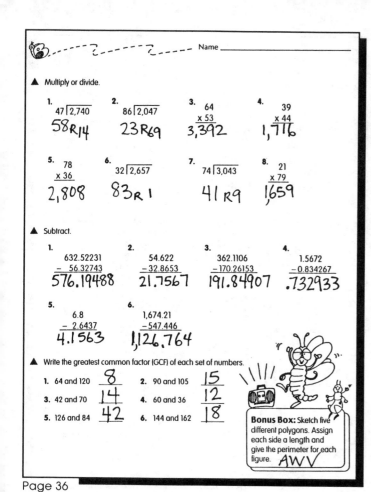

Page 36

Page 37

▲ Use the correct order of operations.

1. $4 \times (24 - 19) + 2 + 3 =$ **13**
2. $2 \times 6 - 21 + 7 =$ **9**
3. $25 + 5 + 5(6 - 2) =$ **6**
4. $100 + (2 \times 6 - 2) =$ **10**
5. $(6 + 8) + 2 \times (4 - 1) =$ **21**
6. $(4 + 5) \times (15 - 9) + 2 =$ **27**
7. $(8 + 4 \times 6) + (9 + 7) =$ **2**
8. $2 + 5 \times 3 + 16 + 2 - 6 =$ **19**

▲ Identify each solid.

1. **pyramid**
2. **cube**
3. **sphere**
4. **cylinder**
5. **cone**

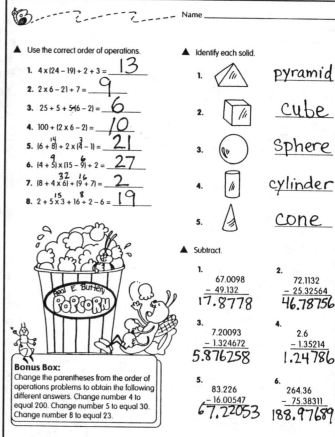

▲ Subtract.

1. $\begin{array}{r} 67.0098 \\ -\ 49.132 \\ \hline \end{array}$ **17.8778**
2. $\begin{array}{r} 72.1132 \\ -\ 25.32564 \\ \hline \end{array}$ **46.78756**
3. $\begin{array}{r} 7.20093 \\ -\ 1.324672 \\ \hline \end{array}$ **5.876258**
4. $\begin{array}{r} 2.6 \\ -\ 1.35214 \\ \hline \end{array}$ **1.24786**
5. $\begin{array}{r} 83.226 \\ -\ 16.00547 \\ \hline \end{array}$ **67.22053**
6. $\begin{array}{r} 264.36 \\ -\ 75.38311 \\ \hline \end{array}$ **188.97689**

Bonus Box: Change the parentheses from the order of operations problems to obtain the following different answers. Change number 4 to equal 200. Change number 5 to equal 30. Change number 8 to equal 23.

Page 37

Page 38

▲ Use the correct order of operations.

1. $(3 + 9) \times 3 + 15 + 5 =$ **30**
2. $(2 \times 3 \times 10 + 4) + (10 - 5 + 3) =$ **8**
3. $2 \times (11 - 3) + (14 - 6 \times 2) =$ **8**
4. $8 + 2 + (5 \times 3 - 5) + 2 =$ **9**
5. $1 \times 6 + 3 + (20 - 2 \times 7) =$ **8**
6. $(16 + 8 + 2) + (6 - 12 + 6) =$ **5**
7. $7 \times 2 \times 5 + (12 - 2) =$ **7**
8. $6 + 12 \times 2 - 8 + 2 + 2 \times 5 =$ **36**

▲ Add or subtract.

1. $\begin{array}{r} 639.253 \\ 2,694.398 \\ +\ 72.8123 \\ \hline \end{array}$ **3,406.4633**
2. $\begin{array}{r} 73.21 \\ -\ 25.24516 \\ \hline \end{array}$ **47.96484**
3. $\begin{array}{r} 2.97 \\ -\ 0.25346 \\ \hline \end{array}$ **2.71654**
4. $\begin{array}{r} 352.977 \\ 4,294.24 \\ +\ 527.6477 \\ \hline \end{array}$ **5,174.8647**

▲ Use front-end estimation to estimate each sum or difference.

1. $\begin{array}{r} 6,352 \\ +\ 2,981 \\ \hline \end{array}$ **9,000**
2. $\begin{array}{r} 7,298,224 \\ -\ 1,734,923 \\ \hline \end{array}$ **5,000,000**
3. $\begin{array}{r} 982,510 \\ -\ 432,516 \\ \hline \end{array}$ **6,1000,000**

4. $\begin{array}{r} 7,892,006 \\ +\ 3,674,997 \\ \hline \end{array}$ **12,000,000**
5. $\begin{array}{r} 416,739 \\ +\ 317,473 \\ \hline \end{array}$ **700,000**
6. $\begin{array}{r} 7,299 \\ -\ 3,176 \\ \hline \end{array}$ **4,000**

1. $3 + (6 \times 3) + 15 \div 5 = 24$

Bonus Box: Change the parentheses from the order of operations problems to obtain the following different answers. Change number 1 to equal 57. Change number 5 to equal 128. Change number 8 to equal 26. *See example above.*

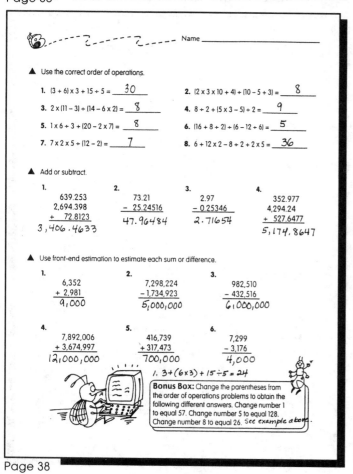

Page 38

Page 39

▲ Use the correct order of operations.

1. $(4 + 8) + 4 + 4 \times 2 =$ **11**
2. $16 - 10 + 2 + (8 + 3) + 3 =$ **20**
3. $5 \times (18 - 9) - 6 \times (2 + 4) =$ **9**
4. $(16 - 10) + 2 - 10 + (2 + 3) =$ **1**
5. $(3 + 6) \times (10 - 6) + 6 =$ **6**
6. $3 \times 1 + 3 + 2 \times (6 - 5) =$ **3**
7. $20 + 5 \times (10 - 3 \times 3) =$ **4**
8. $(11 - 81 + 9) \times (3 + 4) =$ **14**

#1 $4 + 8 \div (4 + 4) \times 2 = 10$
#1 $4 + 8 \div 4 + 4 \times 2 = 14$
#2 $(16 - 10) \div 2 + 18 \div (3 + 3) = 6$

▲ Add or subtract.

1. $\begin{array}{r} 43.8792 \\ +\ 628.3192 \\ \hline \end{array}$ **672.1984**
2. $\begin{array}{r} 152.76 \\ -\ 143.6843 \\ \hline \end{array}$ **9.0757**
3. $\begin{array}{r} 5.708 \\ -\ 2.8999 \\ \hline \end{array}$ **2.8081**
4. $\begin{array}{r} 526.178 \\ +\ 265.9245 \\ \hline \end{array}$ **792.1025**

▲ Multiply or divide.

1. $6 \times 6 =$ **36**
2. $5 \times 7 =$ **35**
3. $49 + 7 =$ **7**
4. $64 + 8 =$ **8**
5. $9 \times 6 =$ **54**
6. $7 \times 8 =$ **56**
7. $24 + 6 =$ **4**
8. $7 \times 9 =$ **63**
9. $21 + 3 =$ **7**
10. $27 + 9 =$ **3**
11. $4 \times 8 =$ **32**
12. $8 \times 6 =$ **48**
13. $54 + 6 =$ **9**
14. $42 + 7 =$ **6**
15. $36 + 4 =$ **9**

Bonus Box: Change the parentheses from the order of operations problems to obtain the following different answers. Change number 1 to equal 10. Change number 1 to equal 14. Change number 2 to equal 6. *See above*

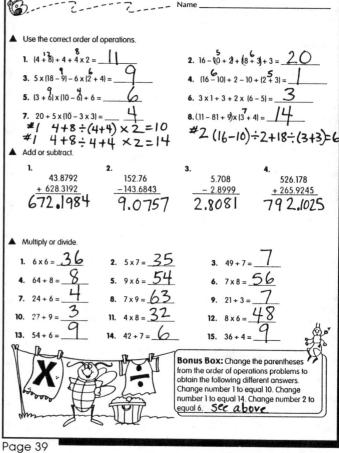

Page 39

Page 40

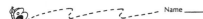

▲ On lined paper, arrange in columns and add. Write the sums here.

1. 4.56 + 21.35 + 3.5783 + 421.55 + 2.39784 = **453.43614**
2. 0.24 + 61.72908 + 31.526 + 6.733 + 2.19807 = **102.42615**
3. 1.62735 + 34.256 + 2.536 + 1.9807 + 32.546 = **72.94605**
4. 65.27 + 0.2537 + 4.1627 + 21.453 + 28.3256 = **119.465**
5. 3.647 + 72.532 + 0.1253 + 6.85934 + 2.5373 = **85.70094**
6. 90.893 + 3.6 + 26.738 + 4.321 + 46.73 + 4.563 = **176.845**

▲ Draw two pictures for each fraction. Illustrate the fraction as part of a whole and then as part of a group. The first one is done for you.

1. $\frac{4}{5}$
2. $\frac{1}{7}$
3. $\frac{3}{8}$
4. $\frac{2}{3}$
5. $\frac{8}{9}$
6. $\frac{5}{9}$

▲ Use the correct order of operations.

1. 12 + 6 − 2 + 1 × 8 + 6 = **14**
2. (16 − 8 + 2) × (3 + 4) − 10 = **74**
3. (10 − 2 × 5) × 16 × 93 = **0**
4. (3 × 3 − 4) × 4 + (2 − 1) = **20**

1. 12 ÷ (6−2) + 1 × (8+6) = 17
2. (16−8) ÷ 2 × 3 + 4 − 10 = 6
4. (3×3−4) × (4÷2+1) = 15

Bonus Box: Change the parentheses from the order of operations problems to obtain the following different answers. Change number 1 to equal 17. Change number 2 to equal 6. Change number 4 to equal 15.

Page 41

▲ Subtract.

1. 23.145 − 0.0087 = **23.1363**
2. 7.835 − 6.0007 = **1.8343**
3. 152.6 − 26.3554 = **126.2446**
4. 16.3744 − 0.009 = **16.3654**
5. 54.6344 − 8.07 = **46.5644**
6. 45.263 − 2.75 = **42.513**

▲ Multiply or divide the numerator and denominator by the same number to make an equivalent fraction. The first one is done for you.

$\frac{3}{5}$ = $\frac{9}{15}$

1. $\frac{3}{5} \times \frac{3}{3} = \frac{9}{15}$
2. $\frac{6}{12} \div \frac{2}{2} = \frac{3}{6}$
3. $\frac{4}{10} \div \frac{2}{2} = \frac{2}{5}$
4. $\frac{1}{3} \times \frac{4}{4} = \frac{4}{12}$
5. $\frac{2}{6} \times \frac{2}{2} = \frac{4}{12}$
6. $\frac{7}{8} \times \frac{2}{2} = \frac{14}{16}$
7. $\frac{10}{12} \div \frac{2}{2} = \frac{5}{6}$
8. $\frac{3}{4} \times \frac{2}{2} = \frac{6}{8}$

▲ Find the area of each figure.

1. 8 m × 8 m = **64** m²
2. 11 m, 6 m = **33** m²
3. 27 m × 44 m = **1,188** m²

Bonus Box: Choose six fractions from above. For each fraction, write two other equivalent fractions. **Answers will vary.**

Page 42

▲ Add or subtract.

1. 5.6 + 3.253 + 12.008 + 35.26 + 0.092001 + 3.3 = **59.513001**
2. 12.460 − 12.362709 = **.097291**
3. 2.00705 − 0.0235167 = **1.9835333**
4. 3.456 + 21.5377 + 0.035 + 46.3522 + 0.008 = **71.3889**

▲ Complete the equivalent fractions.

1. $\frac{2}{6} = \frac{1}{3}$
2. $\frac{5}{20} = \frac{1}{4}$
3. $\frac{6}{7} = \frac{12}{14}$
4. $\frac{2}{7} = \frac{8}{28}$
5. $\frac{6}{8} = \frac{36}{48}$
6. $\frac{5}{9} = \frac{35}{63}$
7. $\frac{21}{49} = \frac{3}{7}$
8. $\frac{1}{3} = \frac{8}{24}$
9. $\frac{4}{5} = \frac{28}{35}$
10. $\frac{2}{3} = \frac{10}{15}$
11. $\frac{12}{16} = \frac{3}{4}$
12. $\frac{4}{6} = \frac{16}{24}$

▲ Write the value of the underlined digit. The first one is done for you.

1. 574,3̲89,002 — eighty thousand
2. 923,5̲10,367 — **three million**
3. 251,627,8̲33 — **eight hundred**
4. 72,8̲93,271 — **800 thousand**
5. 4,2̲98,781,254 — **eight million**
6. 563,3̲34,908 — **60 million**

Bonus Box: Write the above six number words in order from least to greatest. **#3,1,4,2,5,6**

Page 43

▲ Add or subtract.

1. 7.45 + 82.1209 + 3.264 + 33.23348 + 6.35 = **132.41838**
2. 4.608 − 2.463754 = **2.144246**
3. 2.425 − 0.0087653 = **2.4162347**
4. 55.2537 + 2.51667 + 0.112113 + 46.3 + 4.4 = **108.582483**

▲ Simplify each fraction to lowest terms. The first one is done for you.

1. $\frac{3}{12} = \frac{1}{4}$
2. $\frac{12}{18} = \frac{2}{3}$
3. $\frac{32}{40} = \frac{4}{5}$
4. $\frac{27}{33} = \frac{9}{11}$
5. $\frac{48}{56} = \frac{6}{7}$
6. $\frac{7}{21} = \frac{1}{3}$
7. $\frac{36}{63} = \frac{4}{7}$
8. $\frac{56}{63} = \frac{8}{9}$
9. $\frac{8}{20} = \frac{2}{5}$
10. $\frac{42}{48} = \frac{7}{8}$
11. $\frac{21}{28} = \frac{3}{4}$
12. $\frac{35}{49} = \frac{5}{7}$

▲ Write the value of the underlined digit. The first one is done for you.

1. 7,8̲94,343,263 — eight hundred million
2. 426,8̲93 — **ninety**
3. 9,219,8̲07,235 — **eight hundred thousand**
4. 23,516,73̲8,543 — **thirty thousand**
5. 355,638,2̲34 — **50 million**
6. 947,382,3̲76 — **three hundred**

Bonus Box: Choose four numbers from above. Write them in expanded form. **AWV**

Page 44

▲ Multiply.

1. 246 × 7 = 1,722
2. 268 × 9 = 2,412
3. 432 × 6 = 2,592
4. 314 × 2 = 628
5. 621 × 5 = 3,105

6. 853 × 3 = 2,559
7. 743 × 8 = 5,944
8. 830 × 4 = 3320
9. 946 × 5 = 4,730
10. 362 × 7 = 2,534

▲ Simplify each fraction to lowest terms.

1. $\frac{25}{45} = \frac{5}{9}$
2. $\frac{18}{21} = \frac{6}{7}$
3. $\frac{6}{48} = \frac{1}{8}$
4. $\frac{14}{63} = \frac{2}{9}$
5. $\frac{46}{92} = \frac{1}{2}$
6. $\frac{12}{20} = \frac{3}{5}$
7. $\frac{8}{10} = \frac{4}{5}$
8. $\frac{36}{40} = \frac{9}{10}$
9. $\frac{9}{12} = \frac{3}{4}$
10. $\frac{12}{21} = \frac{4}{7}$
11. $\frac{4}{12} = \frac{1}{3}$
12. $\frac{36}{42} = \frac{6}{7}$

▲ Record the perimeter of each figure.

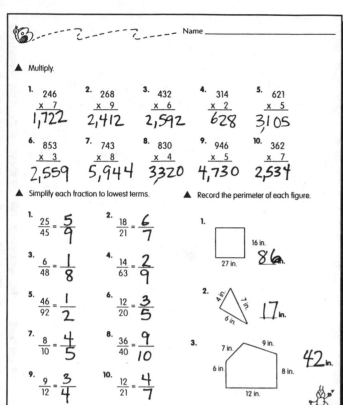

1. 16 in. / 27 in. → 86 in.
2. 4 in. / 7 in. / 6 in. → 17 in.
3. 9 in. / 7 in. / 6 in. / 8 in. / 12 in. → 42 in.

Bonus Box: Write five numbers with less than ten digits so that the digits in each number have a sum of 40. AWV

Page 45

▲ Multiply.

1. 352 × 4 = 1,408
2. 673 × 2 = 1,346
3. 708 × 9 = 6,372
4. 256 × 6 = 1,536
5. 824 × 3 = 2,472

6. 518 × 5 = 2,590
7. 472 × 6 = 2,832
8. 269 × 8 = 2,152
9. 486 × 7 = 3,402
10. 675 × 5 = 3,375

▲ Rename each fraction as a mixed or whole number. The first one is done for you.

1. $\frac{7}{3} = 2\frac{1}{3}$
2. $\frac{24}{5} = 4\frac{4}{5}$
3. $\frac{15}{2} = 7\frac{1}{2}$
4. $\frac{24}{4} = 6$
5. $\frac{35}{4} = 8\frac{3}{4}$
6. $\frac{23}{7} = 3\frac{2}{7}$
7. $\frac{50}{9} = 5\frac{5}{9}$
8. $\frac{17}{6} = 2\frac{5}{6}$

▲ On lined paper, arrange in columns and add. Record the sums here.

1. 5,637 + 89 + 243 + 891 + 4,553 + 74 + 372 = 11,859
2. 902 + 654 + 3,995 + 45 + 721 + 88 + 39 + 536 = 6,980
3. 68 + 432 + 1,894 + 79 + 245 + 426 + 7,350 = 10,494

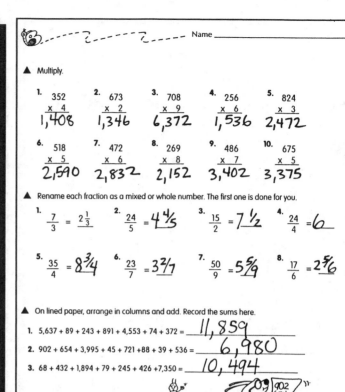

Bonus Box: Write six numbers that when rounded to the nearest tenth, round to 243.8. Include numbers that round up and numbers that round down. AWV

Page 46

▲ Multiply.

1. 536 × 27 = 14,472
2. 604 × 18 = 10,872
3. 451 × 41 = 18,491
4. 846 × 39 = 32,994
5. 524 × 26 = 13,624
6. 627 × 53 = 33,231
7. 892 × 34 = 30,328
8. 931 × 29 = 26,999

▲ Rename each fraction as a mixed or whole number.

1. $\frac{17}{4} = 4\frac{1}{4}$
2. $\frac{16}{2} = 8$
3. $\frac{46}{5} = 9\frac{1}{5}$
4. $\frac{23}{6} = 3\frac{5}{6}$
5. $\frac{18}{7} = 2\frac{4}{7}$
6. $\frac{17}{3} = 5\frac{2}{3}$
7. $\frac{17}{9} = 1\frac{8}{9}$
8. $\frac{12}{3} = 4$

▲ Add.

1. 35.2635 + 3,256.229 + 399.5896 = 3,691.0821
2. 3.25617 + 35.72897 + 0.892313 = 39.877453
3. 5.4737 + 7.278354 + 82.46735 = 95.219404
4. 76.37 + 0.68362 + 61.3785 = 138.43212

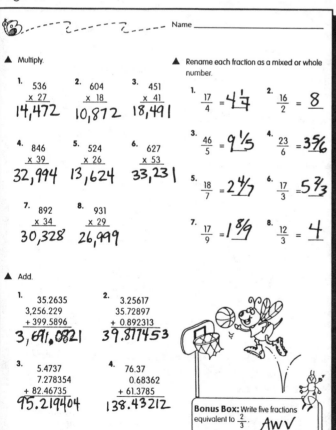

Bonus Box: Write five fractions equivalent to $\frac{2}{3}$. AWV

Page 47

▲ Multiply.

1. 427 × 57 = 24,339
2. 836 × 49 = 40,964
3. 632 × 66 = 41,712
4. 518 × 27 = 13,986
5. 942 × 15 = 14,130

6. 643 × 74 = 47,582
7. 782 × 81 = 63,342
8. 385 × 42 = 16,170
9. 468 × 65 = 30,420
10. 563 × 73 = 41,099

▲ Rename each as an improper fraction.

1. $2\frac{3}{5} = \frac{13}{5}$
2. $4\frac{7}{8} = \frac{39}{8}$
3. $6\frac{1}{2} = \frac{13}{2}$
4. $8\frac{2}{3} = \frac{26}{3}$
5. $5\frac{3}{4} = \frac{23}{4}$
6. $7\frac{1}{3} = \frac{22}{3}$
7. $3\frac{5}{6} = \frac{23}{6}$
8. $4\frac{1}{4} = \frac{17}{4}$

▲ Add or subtract.

1. 6.77 + 2.0093 + 42.553 + 3.64708 + 0.002435 = 54.981815
2. 5.621 − 2.78390233 = 2.8370977
3. 0.9278 + 4.36277 + 3.462 + 6.37453 + 6.63 = 21.7571
4. 72.34 − 66.284315 = 6.055685

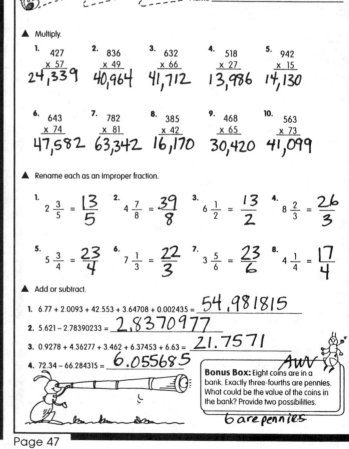

Bonus Box: Eight coins are in a bank. Exactly three-fourths are pennies. What could be the value of the coins in the bank? Provide two possibilities. AWV

6 are pennies

Page 48

▲ Multiply.

1. $924 \times 33 = 30{,}492$
2. $426 \times 46 = 19{,}596$
3. $623 \times 52 = 32{,}396$
4. $552 \times 37 = 20{,}424$
5. $826 \times 12 = 9{,}912$
6. $638 \times 69 = 44{,}022$
7. $314 \times 87 = 27{,}318$
8. $147 \times 68 = 9{,}996$
9. $475 \times 83 = 39{,}425$

▲ Rename each as an improper fraction.

1. $5\frac{4}{7} = \frac{39}{7}$
2. $1\frac{4}{9} = \frac{13}{9}$
3. $2\frac{3}{4} = \frac{11}{4}$
4. $8\frac{2}{3} = \frac{26}{3}$
5. $6\frac{1}{4} = \frac{25}{4}$
6. $9\frac{1}{2} = \frac{19}{2}$
7. $3\frac{4}{5} = \frac{19}{5}$
8. $2\frac{5}{8} = \frac{21}{8}$

▲ Add or subtract.

1. $4.36 + 2.678 + 46.8379 = 53.8759$
2. $4.567 - 3.647833 = .919167$
3. $3.2876 + 25.873 + 38.92083 = 68.08143$
4. $46.89 + 0.52617 + 78.9263 = 126.34247$

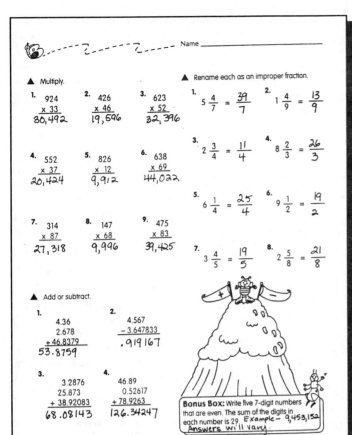

Bonus Box: Write five 7-digit numbers that are even. The sum of the digits in each number is 29. Example – 9,453,152 Answers will vary

Page 49

▲ Divide.

1. $6\overline{)2{,}736} = 456$
2. $8\overline{)5{,}144} = 643$
3. $2\overline{)1{,}834} = 917$
4. $7\overline{)3{,}983} = 569$
5. $5\overline{)3{,}540} = 708$
6. $9\overline{)4{,}239} = 471$

▲ Add the fractions.

1. $\frac{1}{5} + \frac{3}{5} = \frac{4}{5}$
2. $\frac{4}{6} + \frac{1}{6} = \frac{5}{6}$
3. $\frac{1}{3} + \frac{1}{3} = \frac{2}{3}$
4. $\frac{5}{8} + \frac{2}{8} = \frac{7}{8}$

▲ Simplify each fraction to lowest terms.

1. $\frac{12}{8} = \frac{3}{2}\ 1\frac{1}{2}$
2. $\frac{15}{27} = \frac{5}{9}$
3. $\frac{42}{48} = \frac{7}{8}$
4. $\frac{28}{35} = \frac{4}{5}$
5. $\frac{18}{63} = \frac{2}{7}$
6. $\frac{23}{46} = \frac{1}{2}$
7. $\frac{48}{88} = \frac{6}{11}$
8. $\frac{18}{24} = \frac{3}{4}$

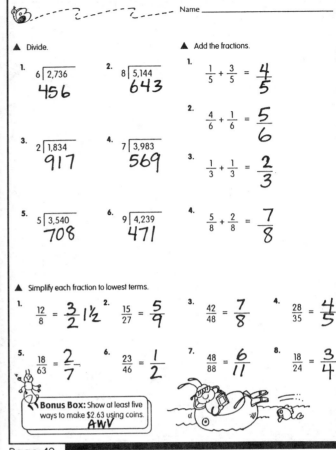

Bonus Box: Show at least five ways to make $2.63 using coins. AWV

Page 50

▲ Divide.

1. $5\overline{)3{,}717} = 743\ R.2$
2. $9\overline{)3{,}678} = 408\ R.6$
3. $4\overline{)2{,}536} = 634$
4. $8\overline{)2{,}181} = 272\ R.5$
5. $3\overline{)2{,}614} = 871\ R.1$
6. $6\overline{)1{,}186} = 197\ R.4$
7. $7\overline{)2{,}564} = 366\ R.2$
8. $9\overline{)5{,}162} = 573\ R.5$

▲ Add the fractions. Simplify each sum to lowest terms. The first one is done for you.

1. $\frac{1}{6} + \frac{2}{6} = \frac{2}{6} = \frac{1}{2}$
2. $\frac{3}{10} + \frac{5}{10} = \frac{8}{10} = \frac{4}{5}$
3. $\frac{4}{9} + \frac{2}{9} = \frac{6}{9} = \frac{2}{3}$
4. $\frac{5}{12} + \frac{5}{12} = \frac{10}{12} = \frac{5}{6}$
5. $\frac{1}{4} + \frac{1}{4} = \frac{2}{4} = \frac{1}{2}$
6. $\frac{3}{16} + \frac{5}{16} = \frac{8}{16} = \frac{1}{2}$

▲ Write the greatest common factor of each set of numbers.

1. 140 and 120 20
2. 84 and 231 21
3. 315 and 60 15
4. 40 and 168 8
5. 270 and 180 90
6. 168 and 189 21

Bonus Box: Sketch five different rectangles. Assign each side a length and give the area for each figure. Answers will vary.

Page 51

▲ Divide.

1. $46\overline{)16{,}192} = 352$
2. $27\overline{)18{,}468} = 684$
3. $59\overline{)25{,}429} = 431$
4. $83\overline{)61{,}918} = 746$
5. $78\overline{)48{,}438} = 621$
6. $65\overline{)53{,}040} = 816$

▲ Add the fractions. Reduce each sum to simplest terms. The first one is done for you.

1. $\frac{5}{14} + \frac{3}{14} = \frac{8}{14} = \frac{4}{7}$
2. $\frac{1}{6} + \frac{3}{6} = \frac{4}{6} = \frac{2}{3}$
3. $\frac{7}{18} + \frac{2}{18} = \frac{9}{18} = \frac{1}{2}$
4. $\frac{4}{10} + \frac{1}{10} = \frac{5}{10} = \frac{1}{2}$
5. $\frac{1}{8} + \frac{1}{8} = \frac{2}{8} = \frac{1}{4}$
6. $\frac{5}{24} + \frac{3}{24} = \frac{8}{24} = \frac{1}{3}$

▲ Use the chart to answer the questions.

Fifth Graders in Clubs			
Club Name	Drama	Chess	Spanish	Technology
# of Students	36	21	48	63

- Which club has 21 members? chess club
- How many fifth graders are in the drama club? 36
- What is the total club membership? 168 students
- Which club has the greatest number of members? technology club

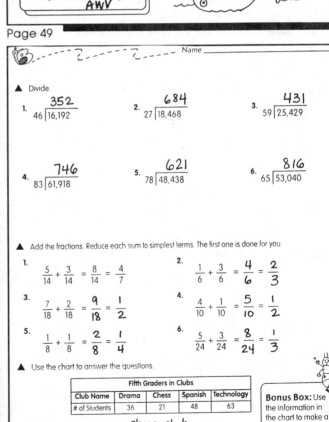

Bonus Box: Use the information in the chart to make a pictograph. Make a key with a symbol that stands for three students. Answers will vary

Page 52

▲ Divide.

1. 21 ⟌ 13,272 = **632**

2. 49 ⟌ 23,569 = **481**

3. 73 ⟌ 23,579 = **323**

4. 74 ⟌ 26,566 = **359**

5. 85 ⟌ 60,605 = **713**

6. 16 ⟌ 2,368 = **148**

▲ Add the fractions. Simplify each sum to lowest terms.

1. $\frac{3}{12} + \frac{6}{12} = \frac{9}{12} = \frac{3}{4}$

2. $\frac{3}{6} + \frac{1}{6} = \frac{4}{6} = \frac{2}{3}$

3. $\frac{13}{18} + \frac{2}{18} = \frac{15}{18} = \frac{5}{6}$

4. $\frac{7}{10} + \frac{1}{10} = \frac{8}{10} = \frac{4}{5}$

5. $\frac{5}{14} + \frac{3}{14} = \frac{8}{14} = \frac{4}{7}$

6. $\frac{1}{8} + \frac{5}{8} = \frac{6}{8} = \frac{3}{4}$

▲ Refer to the chart to answer the questions.

Movies Watched by Fifth- and Sixth-Grade Students				
Week	Comedy	Horror	Romance	Action
1	72	56	24	66
2	48	72	13	84
3	65	90	31	74
4	52	89	35	97

• What is the total number of movies watched in week three? **260 movies**

• How many horror movies were watched during the four weeks? **307 movies**

• In which week were the fewest movies watched? **Week 2 (217)**

• Which type of movie was watched the most? **action movies**

Bonus Box: The school purchases two bottles of glue for every 5 people. How many bottles of glue are purchased if there are 45 students? 150 students? 260 students?

·18 for 45
·60 for 150
·104 for 260

Page 53

▲ Divide.

1. 94 ⟌ 40,984 = **436**

2. 27 ⟌ 19,170 = **710**

3. 46 ⟌ 5,934 = **129**

4. 19 ⟌ 17,898 = **942**

5. 38 ⟌ 21,508 = **566**

6. 83 ⟌ 22,659 = **273**

▲ Add the fractions. Simplify each sum to lowest terms.

1. $\frac{3}{16} + \frac{5}{16} + \frac{2}{16} = \frac{10}{16} = \frac{5}{8}$

2. $\frac{2}{15} + \frac{7}{15} + \frac{1}{15} = \frac{10}{15} = \frac{2}{3}$

3. $\frac{1}{8} + \frac{2}{8} + \frac{3}{8} = \frac{6}{8} = \frac{3}{4}$

4. $\frac{4}{10} + \frac{1}{10} + \frac{3}{10} = \frac{8}{10} = \frac{4}{5}$

5. $\frac{6}{20} + \frac{5}{20} + \frac{1}{20} = \frac{12}{20} = \frac{3}{5}$

6. $\frac{2}{9} + \frac{1}{9} + \frac{3}{9} = \frac{6}{9} = \frac{2}{3}$

▲ Refer to the chart to answer the questions.

Plant Height in Inches				
Plant	Week 1	Week 2	Week 3	Week 4
A	0	$\frac{1}{4}$	$1\frac{1}{16}$	$4\frac{3}{4}$
B	$\frac{1}{16}$	$\frac{1}{2}$	1	$5\frac{3}{16}$

• How much did plant A grow each week?
Week 1 **0** Week 2 **1/4** Week 3 **13/16**
Week 4 **3"/16** inches

• How much did plant B grow each week?
Week 1 **16** Week 2 **7/16** Week 3 **1/2**
Week 4 **43/16** inches

Bonus Box: Draw the actual heights of the two plants each of the four weeks. Organize and label your drawings.

Page 54

▲ Divide.

1. 39 ⟌ 9,610 = **246 R16**

2. 97 ⟌ 54,575 = **562 R61**

3. 41 ⟌ 28,416 = **693 R3**

4. 69 ⟌ 55,498 = **804 R22**

5. 84 ⟌ 61,395 = **730 R75**

6. 52 ⟌ 44,880 = **863 R4**

▲ Subtract the fractions. Simplify to lowest terms. The first one is done for you.

1. $\frac{11}{12} - \frac{5}{12} = \frac{6}{12} = \frac{1}{2}$

2. $\frac{4}{9} - \frac{1}{9} = \frac{3}{9} = \frac{1}{3}$

3. $\frac{7}{16} - \frac{1}{16} = \frac{6}{16} = \frac{3}{8}$

4. $\frac{9}{10} - \frac{3}{10} = \frac{6}{10} = \frac{3}{5}$

5. $\frac{19}{21} - \frac{5}{21} = \frac{14}{21} = \frac{2}{3}$

6. $\frac{4}{6} - \frac{1}{6} = \frac{3}{6} = \frac{1}{2}$

▲ Record the volume of each figure.

1. 3 ft, 9 ft, 2 ft → **54** ft.³

2. 20 mm, 46 mm, 32 mm → **29,440** mm³

3. 12 yds, 6 yds, 6 yds → **432** yd.³

4. 2 cm, 7 cm, 14 cm → **196** cm³

Bonus Box: The swimming pool provides 3 towels for every 7 students. How many towels do they need if there are 56 students? 133 students? 259 students?

24 for 56 st.   57 for 133 st.
111 for 259 st.

Page 55

▲ Divide.

1. 61 ⟌ 56,486 = **926**

2. 48 ⟌ 27,421 = **571 R13**

3. 16 ⟌ 7,720 = **482 R8**

4. 79 ⟌ 27,270 = **345 R15**

5. 39 ⟌ 23,908 = **613 R1**

6. 60 ⟌ 29,300 = **488 R20**

▲ Subtract the fractions. Simplify to lowest terms.

1. $\frac{5}{8} - \frac{3}{8} = \frac{2}{8} = \frac{1}{4}$

2. $\frac{7}{12} - \frac{1}{12} = \frac{6}{12} = \frac{1}{2}$

3. $\frac{3}{4} - \frac{1}{4} = \frac{2}{4} = \frac{1}{2}$

4. $\frac{17}{20} - \frac{5}{20} = \frac{12}{20} = \frac{3}{5}$

5. $\frac{11}{14} - \frac{3}{14} = \frac{8}{14} = \frac{4}{7}$

6. $\frac{8}{9} - \frac{2}{9} = \frac{6}{9} = \frac{2}{3}$

▲ Record the volume of each figure.

1. 13m, 6m, 23m → **1,794** m³ AWV

2. 2m, 4m, 12m → **96** m³

3. 16cm, 16cm, 16cm → **4096** cm³

Bonus Box: Six coins are in a bank. Exactly one third are dimes. What could be the value of the coins in the bank? Provide two possibilities. **2 are dimes**

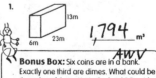

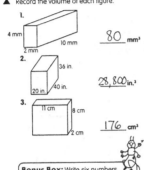

Page 56

Name _____

▲ Multiply or divide.

1. 697 × 68 = 47,396

2. 86)50,830 = 591 R.4

3. 28)13,216 = 472

4. 364 × 73 = 26,572

5. 64)57,156 = 893 R.4

6. 71)24,995 = 352 R.3

▲ Subtract the fractions. Simplify to lowest terms.

1. $2\frac{3}{4} - 1\frac{1}{4} = 1\frac{1}{2}$

2. $5\frac{5}{6} - 2\frac{1}{6} = 3\frac{2}{3}$

3. $7\frac{7}{10} - 5\frac{2}{10} = 2\frac{1}{2}$

4. $3\frac{6}{7} - 1\frac{5}{7} = 2\frac{1}{7}$

5. $4\frac{13}{14} - 1\frac{3}{14} = 3\frac{5}{7}$

6. $8\frac{2}{3} - 4\frac{1}{3} = 4\frac{1}{3}$

▲ Record the volume of each figure.

1. (4 mm, 2 mm, 10 mm) = 80 mm³

2. (36 in., 20 in., 40 in.) = 28,800 in.³

3. (11 cm, 8 cm, 2 cm) = 176 cm³

Bonus Box: Write six numbers that when rounded to the nearest hundredth, round to 354.29. Include numbers that round up and numbers that round down. Answers will vary.

Page 56

Page 57

Name _____

▲ Multiply or divide.

1. 241 × 96 = 23,136

2. 73)37,100 = 508 R16

3. 62)14,635 = 236 R3

4. 355 × 88 = 31,240

5. 39)22,485 = 576 R21

6. 46)43,342 = 942 R10

▲ Add or subtract the fractions. Simplify each answer to lowest terms.

1. $5\frac{7}{9} - 2\frac{4}{9} = 3\frac{1}{3}$

2. $2\frac{1}{6} + 5\frac{2}{6} = 7\frac{1}{2}$

3. $4\frac{5}{10} + 3\frac{3}{10} = 7\frac{4}{5}$

4. $9\frac{7}{12} - 3\frac{3}{12} = 6\frac{1}{3}$

5. $2\frac{5}{14} + 4\frac{3}{14} = 6\frac{4}{7}$

6. $9\frac{3}{4} - 5\frac{1}{4} = 4\frac{1}{2}$

▲ Use the correct order of operations.

1. 4 × (2 − 2) + 8 + 4 = 2

2. (2 + 5 − 1) × 6 − 10 + 2 = 31

3. (8 − 6 + 2) × (12 + 2 − 4) = 10

4. 18 − 5 × 2 + 3 × 6 + 2 = 17

5. (2 + 6) + 4 × 2 + 10 = 14

6. 6 × 5 + 10 − 8 + (2 + 2) = 1

#3 (8−6)÷2×12−(2+4)

#4 (18−5)×2+3×6÷2

Bonus Box: Change the parentheses from the order of operations problems to obtain the following different answers. Change number 3 to equal 6. Change number 4 to equal 35.

Page 57

Page 58

Name _____

▲ Multiply.

1. 23.1 × 4.6 = 106.26

2. 6.19 × .05 = .3095

3. 8.06 × 74 = 596.44

4. .097 × .88 = .08536

5. 9.35 × .37 = 3.4595

6. 8.94 × .06 = .5364

7. .048 × 8.3 = .3984

8. 371 × .32 = 118.72

▲ Add the fractions. Write each answer as a mixed numeral. simplify to lowest terms. The first one is done for you.

1. $\frac{7}{9} + \frac{4}{9} = 1\frac{1}{2}$

2. $\frac{2}{3} + \frac{2}{3} = 1\frac{1}{3}$

3. $\frac{9}{10} + \frac{7}{10} = 1\frac{3}{5}$

4. $\frac{1}{2} + \frac{5}{2} = 3$

5. $\frac{7}{3} + \frac{2}{3} = 3$

6. $\frac{5}{6} + \frac{4}{6} = 1\frac{1}{2}$

▲ Refer to the chart to answer the questions.

• How many students were polled? 290

• Which type of location had the most students? beach

• How many more students stayed home than went skiing? 22

• What fraction of students went to an amusement park? Give your answer in simplest terms. 58/290 = 1/5

Spring Vacation Destinations

Type of Location	# of Students
home	68
beach	79
amusement park	58
skiing	46
other	39

Bonus Box: Show at least five ways to make $3.46 using coins. AWV

Page 58

Page 59

Name _____

▲ Multiply.

1. 7.62 × .09 = .6858

2. .642 × 67 = 43.014

3. 59.1 × .22 = 13.002

4. .005 × .04 = .0002

5. 6.75 × .98 = 6.615

6. 6.87 × 5.1 = 35.037

7. 6.02 × 6.8 = 40.936

8. 217 × 6.9 = 1497.3

9. 4.77 × .04 = .1908

10. 1.06 × 2.3 = 2.438

▲ Add the fractions. Simplify to lowest terms.

1. $2\frac{1}{2} + 5\frac{3}{2} = 9$

2. $4\frac{6}{15} + 1\frac{4}{15} = 5\frac{2}{3}$

3. $1\frac{9}{10} + 2\frac{9}{10} = 4\frac{4}{5}$

4. $5\frac{2}{3} + 6\frac{1}{3} = 12$

5. $3\frac{7}{8} + 7\frac{5}{8} = 11\frac{1}{2}$

6. $3\frac{4}{5} + 5\frac{3}{5} = 9\frac{2}{5}$

▲ Write the numeral for each number word.

1. One hundred forty-five billion, sixty-seven
145,000,000,067

2. Two hundred fifty-one thousandths
.251

3. Six hundred seven billion, sixty-four million, six hundred thirteen and thirty-two ten-thousandths
607,064,000,613.0032

4. Fourteen and five hundred eight thousandths
14.508

Bonus Box: Write five numbers with seven digits each. The digits in each number have a sum of 39. Answers will vary.

Page 59

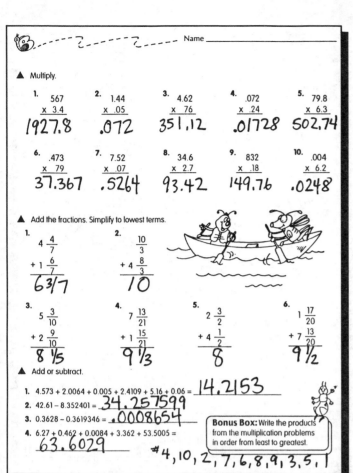

Page 60

▲ Multiply.

1. $567 \times 3.4 = 1927.8$
2. $1.44 \times .05 = .072$
3. $4.62 \times 76 = 351.12$
4. $.072 \times .24 = .01728$
5. $79.8 \times 6.3 = 502.74$

6. $.473 \times 79 = 37.367$
7. $7.52 \times .07 = .5264$
8. $34.6 \times 2.7 = 93.42$
9. $832 \times .18 = 149.76$
10. $.004 \times 6.2 = .0248$

▲ Add the fractions. Simplify to lowest terms.

1. $4\frac{4}{7} + 1\frac{6}{7} = 6\frac{3}{7}$
2. $\frac{10}{3} + 4\frac{8}{3} = 10$
3. $5\frac{3}{10} + 2\frac{9}{10} = 8\frac{1}{5}$
4. $7\frac{13}{21} + 1\frac{15}{21} = 9\frac{1}{3}$
5. $2\frac{3}{2} + 4\frac{1}{2} = 8$
6. $1\frac{17}{20} + 7\frac{13}{20} = 9\frac{1}{2}$

▲ Add or subtract.

1. $4.573 + 2.0064 + 0.005 + 2.4109 + 5.16 + 0.06 = \underline{14.2153}$
2. $42.61 - 8.352401 = \underline{34.257599}$
3. $0.3628 - 0.3619346 = \underline{.0008654}$
4. $6.27 + 0.462 + 0.0084 + 3.362 + 53.5005 = \underline{63.6029}$

Bonus Box: Write the products from the multiplication problems in order from least to greatest.
#4, 10, 2, 7, 6, 8, 9, 3, 5, 1

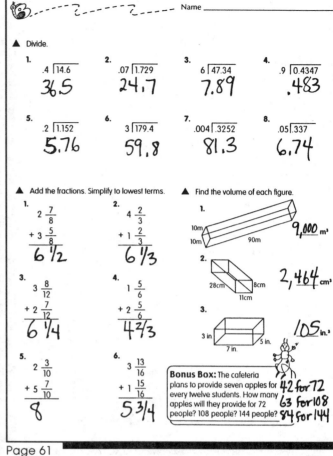

Page 61

▲ Divide.

1. $.4\overline{)14.6} = 36.5$
2. $.07\overline{)1.729} = 24.7$
3. $6\overline{)47.34} = 7.89$
4. $.9\overline{)0.4347} = .483$

5. $.2\overline{)1.152} = 5.76$
6. $3\overline{)179.4} = 59.8$
7. $.004\overline{).3252} = 81.3$
8. $.05\overline{).337} = 6.74$

▲ Add the fractions. Simplify to lowest terms.

1. $2\frac{7}{8} + 3\frac{5}{8} = 6\frac{1}{2}$
2. $4\frac{2}{3} + 1\frac{2}{3} = 6\frac{1}{3}$
3. $3\frac{8}{12} + 2\frac{7}{12} = 6\frac{1}{4}$
4. $1\frac{5}{6} + 2\frac{5}{6} = 4\frac{2}{3}$
5. $2\frac{3}{10} + 5\frac{7}{10} = 8$
6. $3\frac{13}{16} + 1\frac{15}{16} = 5\frac{3}{4}$

▲ Find the volume of each figure.

1. 10m, 10m, 90m — $9,000$ m³
2. 28cm, 8cm, 11cm — $2,464$ cm³
3. 3 in., 7 in., 5 in. — 105 in.³

Bonus Box: The cafeteria plans to provide seven apples for every twelve students. How many apples will they provide for 72 people? 108 people? 144 people?
42 for 72
63 for 108
84 for 144

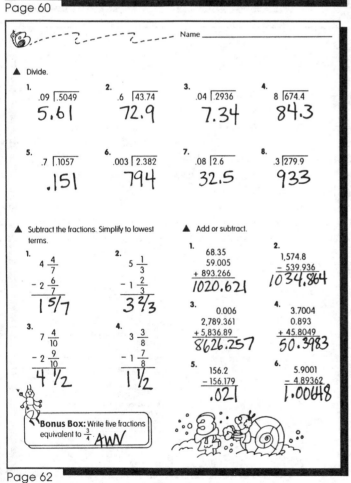

Page 62

▲ Divide.

1. $.09\overline{).5049} = 5.61$
2. $.6\overline{)43.74} = 72.9$
3. $.04\overline{).2936} = 7.34$
4. $8\overline{)674.4} = 84.3$

5. $.7\overline{).1057} = .151$
6. $.003\overline{)2.382} = 794$
7. $.08\overline{)2.6} = 32.5$
8. $.3\overline{)279.9} = 933$

▲ Subtract the fractions. Simplify to lowest terms.

1. $4\frac{4}{7} - 2\frac{6}{7} = 1\frac{5}{7}$
2. $5\frac{1}{3} - 1\frac{2}{3} = 3\frac{2}{3}$
3. $7\frac{4}{10} - 2\frac{9}{10} = 4\frac{1}{2}$
4. $3\frac{3}{8} - 1\frac{7}{8} = 1\frac{1}{2}$

▲ Add or subtract.

1. $68.35 + 59.005 + 893.266 = 1020.621$
2. $1,574.8 - 539.936 = 1034.864$
3. $0.006 + 2,789.361 + 5,836.89 = 8626.257$
4. $3.7004 + 0.893 + 45.8049 = 50.3983$
5. $156.2 - 156.179 = .021$
6. $5.9001 - 4.89362 = 1.00648$

Bonus Box: Write five fractions equivalent to $\frac{3}{4}$. AWV

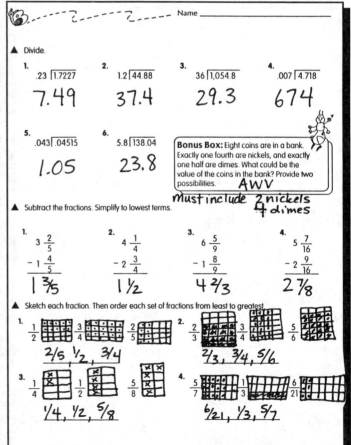

Page 63

▲ Divide.

1. $.23\overline{)1.7227} = 7.49$
2. $1.2\overline{)44.88} = 37.4$
3. $36\overline{)1,054.8} = 29.3$
4. $.007\overline{)4.718} = 674$

5. $.043\overline{).04515} = 1.05$
6. $5.8\overline{)138.04} = 23.8$

Bonus Box: Eight coins are in a bank. Exactly one fourth are nickels, and exactly one half are dimes. What could be the value of the coins in the bank? Provide two possibilities.
AWV
must include 2 nickels 4 dimes

▲ Subtract the fractions. Simplify to lowest terms.

1. $3\frac{2}{5} - 1\frac{4}{5} = 1\frac{3}{5}$
2. $4\frac{1}{4} - 2\frac{3}{4} = 1\frac{1}{2}$
3. $6\frac{5}{9} - 1\frac{8}{9} = 4\frac{2}{3}$
4. $5\frac{7}{16} - 2\frac{9}{16} = 2\frac{7}{8}$

▲ Sketch each fraction. Then order each set of fractions from least to greatest.

1. $\frac{1}{2}$, $\frac{3}{4}$, $\frac{2}{5}$ → 2/5, 1/2, 3/4
2. $\frac{2}{3}$, $\frac{3}{4}$, $\frac{5}{6}$ → 2/3, 3/4, 5/6
3. $\frac{1}{4}$, $\frac{1}{2}$, $\frac{5}{8}$ → 1/4, 1/2, 5/8
4. $\frac{5}{7}$, $\frac{1}{3}$, $\frac{6}{21}$ → 6/21, 1/3, 5/7

118

Page 64

▲ Divide.

1. .053|1.2031 = **22.7**
2. 31|15.128 = **.488**
3. 5.9|32.332 = **5.48**
4. .03|21.54 = **718**

5. .62|2.7962 = **4.51**
6. .0048|.6624 = **138**

Bonus Box: Find and trace twelve angles. Label each right angle, acute angle, or obtuse angle. AWV

▲ Subtract the fractions. Simplify to lowest terms.

1. $5 \frac{7}{10} - 2 \frac{9}{10} =$ **2 4/5**
2. $3 \frac{1}{2} - 1 \frac{2}{2} =$ **1½**
3. $4 \frac{1}{4} - 3 \frac{2}{4} =$ **3/4**
4. $8 \frac{7}{14} - 3 \frac{9}{14} =$ **4 6/7**

▲ Sketch each fraction. Then order each set of fractions from least to greatest.

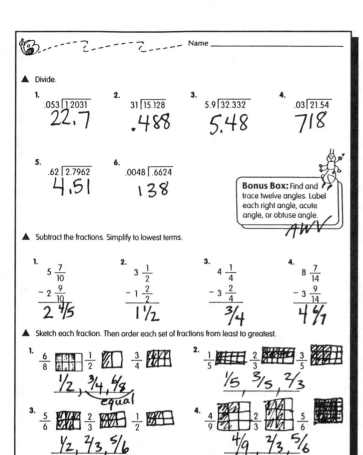

1. $\frac{6}{8}$ $\frac{1}{2}$ $\frac{3}{4}$ → **1/2, 3/4, 6/8 equal**
2. $\frac{1}{5}$ $\frac{2}{5}$ $\frac{3}{5}$ → **1/5, 3/5, 2/3**
3. $\frac{5}{6}$ $\frac{2}{3}$ $\frac{1}{2}$ → **1/2, 2/3, 5/6**
4. $\frac{4}{9}$ $\frac{2}{3}$ $\frac{5}{6}$ → **4/9, 2/3, 5/6**

Page 64

Page 65

▲ Divide.

1. 6.2|12.586 = **2.03**
2. .0091|.48048 = **52.8**
3. .29|.9628 = **3.32**
4. .037|.005698 = **.154**

5. 58|46.168 = **.796**
6. 8.3|549.46 = **66.2**

Bonus Box: The store is selling 3 cookies for 61¢. How much will it cost for 21 cookies? How many cookies can you get for $2.44? **$4.27 12 cookies**

▲ Subtract the fractions. Simplify to lowest terms.

1. $4 \frac{2}{5} - 1 \frac{4}{5} =$ **2 3/5**
2. $7 \frac{3}{14} - 2 \frac{7}{14} =$ **4 5/7**
3. $6 \frac{2}{10} - 4 \frac{8}{10} =$ **1 2/5**
4. $8 \frac{2}{6} - 2 \frac{5}{6} =$ **5 ½**

▲ Write each decimal. Change each decimal to a percent.

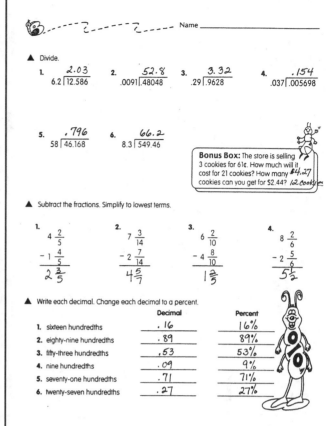

	Decimal	Percent
1. sixteen hundredths	.16	16%
2. eighty-nine hundredths	.89	89%
3. fifty-three hundredths	.53	53%
4. nine hundredths	.09	9%
5. seventy-one hundredths	.71	71%
6. twenty-seven hundredths	.27	27%

Page 65

Page 66

▲ Multiply or divide.

1. 24.1 × 7.2 = **173.52**
2. 4.1|152.11 = **37.1**
3. .039|18.057 = **463**

4. .352 × 6.3 = **2.2176**
5. .0047|.011656 = **2.48**

Bonus Box: Use grid paper to sketch five different shapes with an area of 16. Find the perimeter for each. AWV

▲ Subtract the fractions. Simplify to lowest terms.

1. $3 \frac{1}{2} - 2 \frac{1}{2} =$ **1**
2. $6 \frac{3}{4} - 2 \frac{2}{4} =$ **4 ¼**
3. $4 \frac{2}{9} - 1 \frac{5}{9} =$ **2 2/3**
4. $3 \frac{3}{16} - 1 \frac{7}{16} =$ **1 ¾**

▲ Write each decimal. Change each decimal to a percent.

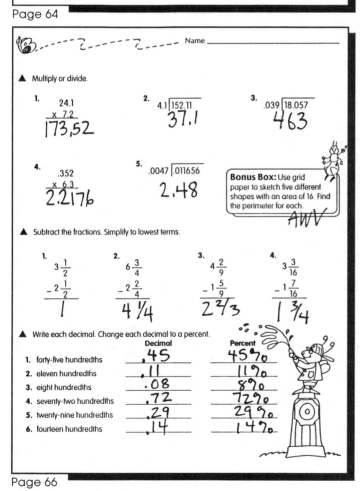

	Decimal	Percent
1. forty-five hundredths	.45	45%
2. eleven hundredths	.11	11%
3. eight hundredths	.08	8%
4. seventy-two hundredths	.72	72%
5. twenty-nine hundredths	.29	29%
6. fourteen hundredths	.14	14%

Page 66

Page 67

▲ Multiply or divide.

1. 4.09 × .09 = **.3681**
2. 69|359.49 = **5.21**
3. .74|5.957 = **8.05**

4. .0056 × 7.8 = **.04368**
5. .24|1.5624 = **6.51**

Bonus Box: Draw models for two of the fractions from the bottom of the page. AWV

▲ Add or subtract the fractions. Simplify to lowest terms.

1. $6 \frac{4}{21} - 2 \frac{18}{21} =$ **3 1/3**
2. $6 \frac{3}{16} - 4 \frac{11}{16} =$ **1 ½**
3. $4 \frac{3}{7} + 1 \frac{6}{7} =$ **6 2/7**
4. $3 \frac{7}{9} + 2 \frac{5}{9} =$ **6 1/3**

▲ Write each decimal. Change each decimal to a percent. Change the percents to fractions. Write the fractions in lowest terms.

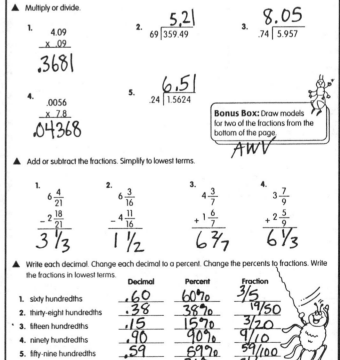

	Decimal	Percent	Fraction
1. sixty hundredths	.60	60%	3/5
2. thirty-eight hundredths	.38	38%	19/50
3. fifteen hundredths	.15	15%	3/20
4. ninety hundredths	.90	90%	9/10
5. fifty-nine hundredths	.59	59%	59/100
6. twenty-one hundredths	.21	21%	21/100

Page 67

Page 68

▲ Multiply or divide.

1.
```
    36.8
  x  27
  993.6
```

2.
```
      9.49
4.2 ) 39.858
```

3.
```
        5.95
.067 ) .39865
```

4.
```
    5.66
  x  .03
   .1698
```

5.
```
        9.52
.068 ) .64736
```

Bonus Box: Write five numbers that have eight digits each. The sum of the digits for each number is 42. The first digit is double the last digit. *Answers will vary.*

▲ Find common denominators. Add the fractions. Simplify to lowest terms. The first one is done for you.

1. $\frac{1}{4} + \frac{1}{2} = \frac{1}{4} + \frac{2}{4} = \frac{3}{4}$

2. $\frac{3}{5} + \frac{2}{3} = 1\frac{4}{15}$

3. $\frac{5}{8} + \frac{1}{4} = \frac{7}{8}$

4. $\frac{3}{10} + \frac{1}{5} = \frac{1}{2}$

▲ Write each decimal. Change each decimal to a percent. Change the percents to fractions. Write the fractions in lowest terms.

	Decimal	Percent	Fraction
1. thirty-nine hundredths	.39	39%	$\frac{39}{100}$
2. two hundredths	.02	2%	$\frac{1}{50}$
3. fifty-one hundredths	.51	51%	$\frac{51}{100}$
4. eighty hundredths	.80	80%	$\frac{4}{5}$
5. twelve hundredths	.12	12%	$\frac{3}{25}$
6. eighty-three hundredths	.83	83%	$\frac{83}{100}$

Page 69

Name _____

▲ Find common denominators. Add the fractions. Simplify to lowest terms.

1. $\frac{2}{3} + \frac{1}{9} = \frac{7}{9}$

2. $\frac{2}{7} + \frac{1}{2} = \frac{11}{14}$

3. $\frac{4}{9} + \frac{1}{6} = \frac{11}{18}$

4. $\frac{1}{6} + \frac{1}{5} = \frac{11}{30}$

5. $\frac{2}{4} + \frac{1}{6} = \frac{2}{3}$

6. $\frac{2}{8} + \frac{1}{7} = \frac{11}{28}$

▲ Find the average of each set of numbers.

1. 456 273 802 321 → 463

2. 5,803 240 4,637 3,672 → 3,588

3. 649 317 253 761 → 495

4. 56 21 79 49 43 28 → 46

5. 21,114 11,314 41,117 → 24,515

6. 99 163 266 290 87 → 181

▲ Write each decimal. Change each decimal to a percent. Change the percents to fractions. Write the fractions in lowest terms.

	Decimal	Percent	Fraction
1. twenty-five hundredths	.25	25%	$\frac{1}{4}$
2. six hundredths	.06	6%	$\frac{3}{50}$
3. seventy-two hundredths	.72	72%	$\frac{18}{25}$
4. twelve hundredths	.12	12%	$\frac{3}{25}$

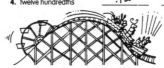

Bonus Box: You can buy 6 carnival tickets for 75¢. How many tickets can you get for $4.50? How much will 54 tickets cost? *54 or 6.75*

Page 70

Name _____

▲ Find common denominators. Add the fractions. Simplify to lowest terms.

1. $\frac{4}{7} + \frac{5}{6} = 1\frac{17}{42}$

2. $\frac{8}{9} + \frac{2}{3} = 1\frac{5}{9}$

3. $\frac{7}{10} + \frac{4}{5} = 1\frac{1}{2}$

4. $\frac{1}{2} + \frac{3}{4} = 1\frac{1}{4}$

5. $\frac{1}{6} + \frac{11}{12} = 1\frac{1}{12}$

6. $\frac{4}{9} + \frac{5}{12} = \frac{31}{36}$

▲ Find the average of each set of numbers.

1. 67 31 52 48 92 → 58

2. 34,675 39,534 32,318 → 35,509

3. 3,415 8,211 6,937 4,605 → 5,792

4. 673 589 342 475 440 475 → 499

5. 67,465 65,472 66,908 → 66,615

6. 366 821 385 336 → 477

▲ Add or subtract.

1.
```
  567.93
   63.721
+ 241.0085
  872.6595
```

2.
```
   3,627.9
 - 3,617.874
   10.026
```

3.
```
     2.635
   256.7289
 + 500.03706
   759.40096
```

4.
```
    0.0034
   35.728
 + 16.8396
   52.5711
```

Bonus Box: Use grid paper to sketch five different shapes with an area of 20. Find the perimeter of each.

Page 71

Name _____

▲ Find common denominators. Add the fractions. Reduce to lowest terms.

1. $\frac{1}{3} + \frac{1}{2} + \frac{3}{4} = 1\frac{7}{12}$

2. $\frac{5}{6} + \frac{3}{4} + \frac{2}{3} = 2\frac{1}{4}$

3. $\frac{3}{8} + \frac{5}{6} + \frac{1}{3} = 1\frac{13}{24}$

4. $\frac{5}{9} + \frac{2}{3} + \frac{1}{6} = 1\frac{7}{18}$

5. $\frac{2}{5} + \frac{7}{10} + \frac{1}{4} = 1\frac{7}{20}$

6. $\frac{3}{7} + \frac{1}{2} + \frac{3}{4} = 1\frac{19}{28}$

▲ Find the mean, mode, median, and range for each set of numbers. Complete the chart.

Set A: 56 72 71 72 67 80 77 72 81
Set B: 14 21 17 23 17 21 17
Set C: 97 100 100 90 92 100 94 91

Set	Mean	Mode	Median	Range
A	72	72	72	25
B	18.57	17	17	9
C	95.5	100	95.5	10

▲ Multiply or divide.

1.
```
   8.09
 x  3.1
 25.079
```

2.
```
        39.8
.56 ) 22.288
```

3.
```
        86.5
.006 ) .519
```

4.
```
    74.8
  x  .02
  1.496
```

Bonus Box: I have 12 coins. Exactly three-fourths are pennies and exactly one-sixth are quarters. What could be the value of my coins? Give two possibilities. *Vary.*

 Name _____

▲ Find common denominators. Subtract the fractions. Simplify to lowest terms.

1. $\frac{5}{6} - \frac{2}{3} = \frac{1}{6}$
2. $\frac{5}{8} - \frac{1}{4} = \frac{3}{8}$
3. $\frac{2}{3} - \frac{4}{7} = \frac{2}{21}$
4. $\frac{3}{5} - \frac{1}{3} = \frac{4}{15}$
5. $\frac{5}{9} - \frac{1}{6} = \frac{7}{18}$
6. $\frac{1}{2} - \frac{3}{8} = \frac{1}{8}$

▲ Find the mean, mode, median, and range for each set of numbers. Complete the chart.

Set A: 35 41 68 35 83
Set B: 5 12 8 16 12 19
Set C: 101 132 100 98 132 124 115 110 132

Set	Mean	Mode	Median	Range
A	52.4	35	41	48
B	12	12	12	14
C	116	132	115	34

▲ Use the correct order of operations.

1. $6 \times (2 + 4) - 10 \div 2 =$ 31
2. $(6 + 10) \div 2 + 14 \div 2 =$ 15
3. $2 \times 5 + 3 \times 6 + 9 =$ 12
4. $2 \times (2 + 1) - 10 + (2 \times 5) =$ 5
5. $(10 - 8) + 2 + (3 + 1) \times 4 =$ 17
6. $16 - 2 \times 2 + 8 + 2 - 0 =$ 16

#1 $6 \times 2 + 4 - 10 \div 2 = 11$
#4 $10 - 8 \div 2 + 3 + 1 \times 4 = 13$

Bonus Box: Change the parentheses from the order of operations problems to obtain the following different answers. Change number 1 to equal 11. Change number 4 to equal 13.

 Name _____

▲ Find common denominators. Subtract the fractions. Simplify to lowest terms.

1. $\frac{1}{2} - \frac{3}{7} = \frac{1}{14}$
2. $\frac{7}{8} - \frac{3}{4} = \frac{1}{8}$
3. $\frac{9}{10} - \frac{4}{5} = \frac{1}{10}$
4. $\frac{4}{7} - \frac{1}{3} = \frac{5}{21}$
5. $\frac{2}{3} - \frac{5}{9} = \frac{1}{9}$
6. $\frac{4}{5} - \frac{1}{4} = \frac{11}{20}$

▲ Find the mean, mode, median, and range for each set of numbers. Complete the chart.

Set A: 16 25 33 17 13 33
Set B: 68 74 99 51 68
Set C: 88 87 89 90 85 88 89

Set	Mean	Mode	Median	Range
A	22.83	33	21	17
B	72	68	68	48
C	88	88 and 89	88	5

▲ Write each decimal. Change each decimal to a percent. Change the percents to fractions. Write the fractions in simplest terms.

	Decimal	Percent	Fraction
1. eight hundredths	.08	8%	2/25
2. forty hundredths	.40	40%	2/5
3. sixty-five hundredths	.65	65%	13/20
4. forty-two hundredths	.42	42%	21/50

Bonus Box: On grid paper, sketch a figure that is 2 by 4 by 3. What is the volume of the figure? What is its surface area? V= 24
surface area = 52

Name _____

▲ Find common denominators. Subtract the fractions. Simplify to lowest terms.

1. $\frac{3}{4} - \frac{2}{3} = \frac{1}{12}$
2. $\frac{7}{9} - \frac{2}{6} = \frac{4}{9}$
3. $\frac{4}{5} - \frac{2}{3} = \frac{2}{15}$
4. $\frac{7}{12} - \frac{2}{4} = \frac{1}{12}$
5. $\frac{1}{6} - \frac{1}{9} = \frac{1}{18}$
6. $\frac{4}{7} - \frac{2}{5} = \frac{6}{35}$

▲ Find the percentage.

1. 25% of 52 = 13
2. 33% of 300 = 99
3. 30% of 80 = 24
4. 2% of 400 = 8
5. 16% of 50 = 8
6. 62% of 50 = 31

▲ Find the volume of each figure.

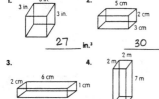

1. 3 in. cube — 27 in.³
2. 5 cm box — 30 cm³
3. — 12 cm³
4. — 28 m³

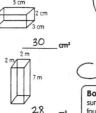

Bonus Box: Find the surface area for each of the four figures above.

 Name _____

▲ Find common denominators. Add the fractions. Simplify to lowest terms.

1. $2 \frac{4}{5} + 3 \frac{2}{3} = 6 \frac{7}{15}$
2. $4 \frac{5}{6} + 1 \frac{3}{4} = 6 \frac{7}{12}$
3. $1 \frac{9}{10} + 3 \frac{3}{5} = 5 \frac{1}{2}$
4. $4 \frac{7}{8} + 5 \frac{1}{2} = 10 \frac{3}{8}$
5. $5 \frac{3}{4} + 2 \frac{5}{8} = 8 \frac{3}{8}$
6. $3 \frac{2}{5} + 2 \frac{3}{4} = 6 \frac{3}{20}$
7. $2 \frac{1}{2} + 2 \frac{6}{7} = 5 \frac{5}{14}$
8. $4 \frac{3}{4} + 2 \frac{2}{3} = 7 \frac{5}{12}$

▲ Find the percentage.

1. 10% of 140 = 14
2. 21% of 100 = 21
3. 15% of 40 = 6
4. 55% of 60 = 33
5. 3% of 200 = 6
6. 80% of 5 = 4

▲ Add or subtract the integers. The first one is done for you.

1. $-4 + +6 =$ +2
2. $-3 + -5 =$ -8
3. $-9 + +2 =$ -7
4. $+3 + -4 =$ -1
5. $-4 - -2 =$ -2
6. $-10 - +5 =$ -15
7. $+6 - +8 =$ -2
8. $+9 - -3 =$ +12

Bonus Box: Write five numbers with four digits each. The digits in each number have a sum of 18. AW

Page 76

▲ Find common denominators. Add the fractions. Simplify to lowest terms.

1. $4\frac{7}{8} + 1\frac{1}{2} = 6\frac{3}{8}$
2. $3\frac{4}{5} + 2\frac{5}{6} = 6\frac{19}{30}$
3. $8\frac{1}{2} + 1\frac{5}{7} = 10\frac{3}{14}$
4. $1\frac{9}{10} + 6\frac{1}{2} = 8\frac{2}{5}$

5. $2\frac{11}{12} + 3\frac{3}{4} = 6\frac{2}{3}$
6. $1\frac{7}{9} + 3\frac{5}{6} = 5\frac{11}{18}$
7. $4\frac{3}{4} + 3\frac{1}{2} = 8\frac{1}{4}$
8. $1\frac{4}{7} + 2\frac{2}{5} = 3\frac{34}{35}$

▲ Find the percentage.

1. 5% of 140 = 7
3. 90% of 60 = 54
5. 8% of 25 = 2
2. 34% of 200 = 68
4. 14% of 150 = 21
6. 70% of 20 = 14

▲ Add or subtract the integers.

1. $-9 - {+3} = -12$
2. $+4 - {+8} = -4$
3. $+2 + {-7} = -5$
4. $+8 - {-10} = +18$
5. $-12 - {-4} = -8$
6. $-4 + {-12} = -16$
7. $-9 - {-15} = +6$
8. $+1 + {+3} = +4$
9. $+13 - {-2} = +15$

Bonus Box: Show at least five ways to make $5.21 using coins.

Page 77

▲ Find common denominators. Add the fractions. Simplify to lowest terms.

1. $2\frac{1}{4} + 1\frac{2}{3} = 3\frac{11}{12}$
2. $6\frac{7}{8} + 3\frac{1}{4} = 10\frac{1}{8}$
3. $2\frac{7}{10} + 4\frac{3}{4} = 7\frac{9}{20}$
4. $2\frac{4}{5} + 1\frac{1}{2} = 4\frac{3}{10}$

5. $3\frac{4}{7} + 2\frac{1}{2} = 6\frac{1}{14}$
6. $2\frac{1}{3} + 3\frac{7}{9} = 6\frac{1}{9}$
7. $1\frac{2}{3} + 5\frac{5}{8} = 7\frac{7}{24}$
8. $2\frac{4}{9} + 4\frac{5}{6} = 7\frac{5}{18}$

▲ There are three ways to write ratios: 5 to 6, 5/6, or 5:6. Write each ratio two other ways.

1. 2 to 3 2/3 2:3
2. 9 to 6 9/6 9:6
3. 7 to 3 7/3 7:3
4. 5 to 9 5/9 5:9
5. 3 to 6 3/6 3:6
6. 8 to 4 8/4 8:4
7. 12 to 9 12/9 12:9
8. 1 to 7 1/7 1:7
9. 8 to 3 8/3 8:3
10. 12 to 5 12/5 12:5

▲ Add or subtract the integers.

1. $-12 + {+5} = -7$
2. $+14 - {+13} = +1$
3. $-8 + {-12} = -20$
4. $-8 - {-11} = +3$
5. $-2 - {+7} = -9$
6. $+10 + {-6} = +4$
7. $+2 + {+4} = +6$
8. $-15 + {+14} = -1$

Bonus Box: Use grid paper to sketch five different shapes with an area of 30. Find the perimeter of each.

Page 78

▲ Find common denominators. Subtract the fractions. Simplify to lowest terms.

1. $3\frac{1}{5} - 1\frac{1}{2} = 1\frac{7}{10}$
2. $6\frac{1}{3} - 4\frac{7}{9} = 1\frac{5}{9}$
3. $4\frac{5}{9} - 1\frac{3}{4} = 2\frac{29}{36}$
4. $8\frac{1}{2} - 5\frac{6}{7} = 2\frac{9}{14}$

5. $7\frac{2}{6} - 2\frac{7}{12} = 4\frac{3}{4}$
6. $9\frac{3}{10} - 4\frac{5}{6} = 4\frac{7}{15}$
7. $5\frac{1}{4} - 1\frac{7}{8} = 3\frac{3}{8}$
8. $2\frac{4}{9} - 1\frac{5}{6} = \frac{11}{18}$

▲ There are three ways to write ratios: 5 to 6, 5/6, or 5:6. Write each ratio two other ways.

1. 6 to 1 6/1 6:1
2. 14 to 3 14/3 14:3
3. 4 to 7 4/7 4:7
4. 2 to 9 2/9 2:9
5. 6 to 11 6/11 6:11
6. 8 to 3 8/3 8:3
7. 15 to 4 15/4 15:4
8. 2 to 10 2/10 2:10
9. 24 to 19 24/19 24:19
10. 51 to 18 51/18 51:18

▲ Write the algebraic expression for each word expression. The first one is done for you.

1. r decreased by 4   r-4
2. y divided by 2   y/2
3. p and 7   p + 7
4. d times 3   d3
5. twelve divided by g   12/g
6. five less than k   k-5

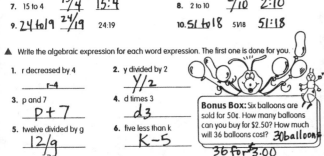

Bonus Box: Six balloons are sold for 50¢. How many balloons can you buy for $2.50? How much will 36 balloons cost?   30 balloons   36 for $3.00

Page 79

▲ Find common denominators. Subtract the fractions. Simplify to lowest terms.

1. $5\frac{1}{2} - 2\frac{5}{6} = 2\frac{2}{3}$
2. $4\frac{2}{5} - 2\frac{7}{10} = 1\frac{7}{10}$
3. $7\frac{1}{9} - 3\frac{5}{6} = 3\frac{5}{18}$
4. $6\frac{1}{8} - 1\frac{2}{6} = 4\frac{19}{24}$

5. $3\frac{3}{10} - 2\frac{1}{2} = \frac{4}{5}$
6. $8\frac{1}{3} - 3\frac{5}{9} = 4\frac{7}{9}$
7. $9\frac{4}{7} - 1\frac{3}{4} = 7\frac{23}{28}$
8. $4\frac{1}{6} - 2\frac{5}{9} = 1\frac{11}{18}$

▲ Draw a model of each ratio.

1. The ratio of red cubes to blue cubes is 3 to 7.
   □□□ — red
   □□□□ □□□ — blue
2. The ratio of subtraction problems to addition problems is 4:1.
   10-2 18-9
   8-5   6-3   5+5
3. The ratio of total books to biographies is 5:2.
   ⬚⬚⬚ ⬚⬚ } biographies
4. The ratio of boys to girls is 1/3.
   boy   girls

▲ Write the algebraic expression for each word expression. The first one is done for you.

1. five more than y   y + 5
2. sixteen minus r   16-r
3. ten divided by p   10/p
4. six times z   6z
5. m divided by 3   m/3
6. four more than b   b+4

Bonus Box: Sketch two 3-dimensional figures. Label the dimensions. Give the volume and surface area for each figure.   AWV

Page 80

▲ Find common denominators. Subtract the fractions. Simplify to lowest terms.

1. $5\frac{4}{7}$ − $2\frac{2}{3}$ = $2\frac{19}{21}$

2. $7\frac{1}{4}$ − $4\frac{1}{3}$ = $2\frac{11}{12}$

3. $9\frac{1}{10}$ − $1\frac{1}{2}$ = $7\frac{3}{5}$

4. $4\frac{1}{3}$ − $2\frac{3}{5}$ = $1\frac{11}{15}$

5. $2\frac{3}{7}$ − $\frac{3}{4}$ = $1\frac{19}{28}$

6. $8\frac{1}{9}$ − $1\frac{1}{3}$ = $6\frac{7}{9}$

7. $7\frac{2}{5}$ − $2\frac{1}{2}$ = $4\frac{9}{10}$

8. $4\frac{5}{12}$ − $3\frac{5}{6}$ = $\frac{7}{12}$

▲ Draw a model of each ratio.

1. The ratio of striped socks to solid-colored socks is 2:6.

2. The ratio of total dots to green dots is 9 to 2.
}green

3. The ratio of candy bars to suckers is 10:1.

4. The ratio of yellow pencils to total pencils is 5:6.
yellow

▲ Write the word expression for each algebraic expression.

1. 6 − g **6 minus g**   2. 4h **4 times h**

3. f + 3 **f plus 3**   4. r/5 **r divided by 5**

5. p − 14 **p minus 14**   6. 4/y **4 divided by y**

Bonus Box: Write five number sentences with an answer of $4\frac{1}{3}$.

AWV

Page 81

▲ Find common denominators. Add or subtract the fractions. Simplify to lowest terms.

1. $2\frac{4}{5}$ + $3\frac{7}{10}$ = $6\frac{1}{2}$

2. $6\frac{1}{2}$ − $1\frac{5}{6}$ = $4\frac{2}{3}$

3. $4\frac{2}{3}$ + $2\frac{5}{9}$ = $7\frac{2}{9}$

4. $6\frac{3}{8}$ − $2\frac{3}{4}$ = $3\frac{5}{8}$

5. $9\frac{5}{7}$ − $4\frac{2}{3}$ = $5\frac{1}{21}$

6. $2\frac{3}{4}$ + $1\frac{5}{6}$ = $4\frac{7}{12}$

7. $5\frac{2}{9}$ − $1\frac{5}{6}$ = $3\frac{7}{18}$

8. $4\frac{1}{2}$ − $2\frac{8}{9}$ = $1\frac{11}{18}$

▲ Circle each set of equivalent ratios. If they are not equivalent, change the second ratio to make them equivalent.

Answers may vary.

1. 4 to 5   8 to 10   2. 6:2   12:4   3. 12/5   ~~6~~ 24/10

4. 3:8   9:24   5. 7/2   ~~14/4~~ 14/4   6. 10 to 3   ~~30 to 9~~

7. 5/11   ~~16/22~~ 10/22   8. 4 to 8   1 to 2   9. 36:6   ~~6:2~~ 6:1

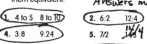

▲ Write the word expression for each algebraic expression.

1. 14 + t **t times 4**   2. 5 + h **5 plus h**

3. r/5 **r divided by 5**   4. w6 **w times 6**

5. q + 2 **q plus 2**

6. 44/f **44 divided by f**   example 983,477

Bonus Box: Write five numbers that have six digits each so that the sum of the digits for each number is 38, the first digit is greater than the second digit, and no digit is zero.

Page 82

▲ Find common denominators. Add or subtract the fractions. Simplify to lowest terms.

1. $4\frac{6}{7}$ + $5\frac{1}{2}$ = $10\frac{5}{14}$

2. $4\frac{2}{3}$ − $2\frac{7}{9}$ = $1\frac{8}{9}$

3. $8\frac{1}{5}$ + $2\frac{2}{3}$ = $10\frac{13}{15}$

4. $3\frac{5}{8}$ + $3\frac{3}{4}$ = $7\frac{3}{8}$

5. $5\frac{1}{2}$ − $2\frac{7}{8}$ = $2\frac{5}{8}$

6. $1\frac{3}{4}$ + $1\frac{5}{6}$ = $3\frac{7}{12}$

7. $3\frac{4}{9}$ − $1\frac{5}{6}$ = $1\frac{11}{18}$

8. $6\frac{1}{10}$ − $2\frac{1}{2}$ = $3\frac{3}{5}$

▲ Circle each set of equivalent ratios. If they are not equivalent, change the second ratio to make them equivalent.

1. 5:6   ~~15:12~~ 15:18   2. 3/1   9/3   3. 4 to 7   12 to 17   12 to 21

4. 6/2   ~~4/1~~ 3/1   5. 9 to 3   30 to 10   6. 8:5   40:25

7. 2:6   1:4   1:3   8. 15/6   ~~5/3~~ 5/2   9. 1 to 4   4 to 16

▲ Solve each algebraic expression for the given values. The first one has been done for you.

1. Solve 2g
if g = 2.45 **4.9**   if g = 34 **68**   if g = 0.086 **.172**

2. Solve h − 3.465
if h = 4.02 **.555**   if h = 56 **52.535**   if h = 6.3 **2.835**

A.W.V.
must have
6 pennies
4 nickels

Bonus Box: Twelve coins are in a bank. Exactly one half are pennies, and exactly one third are nickels. What could be the value of the coins in the bank? Provide two possibilities.

Page 83

▲ Find the products. Simplify to lowest terms. The first one is done for you.

1. $\frac{1}{3} \times \frac{6}{7} = \frac{6}{21} = \frac{2}{7}$

2. $\frac{2}{5} \times \frac{15}{16} = \frac{3}{8}$

3. $\frac{5}{6} \times \frac{3}{5} = \frac{1}{2}$

4. $\frac{4}{9} \times \frac{3}{4} = \frac{1}{3}$

▲ Refer to the table to calculate the relative frequency of each event. Write as a ratio. The first one is done for you.

Purchases at Movie Night

Grade	Popcorn	Trail Mix	# of Students
Fifth	70	25	95
Sixth	30	50	80
Seventh	45	55	100

What is the relative frequency of . . .

1. a sixth grader purchasing trail mix? **50:80**

2. a fifth grader purchasing popcorn? **70:95**

3. a seventh grader purchasing trail mix? **55:100**

4. a fifth or seventh grader purchasing popcorn? **115:195**

5. a sixth or seventh grader purchasing trail mix? **105:180**

6. a fifth, sixth, or seventh grader purchasing popcorn? **145:275**

▲ Solve each algebraic expression for the given values.

1. Solve r ÷ 2.2
if r = 79.2 **36**   if r = 3.3 **1.5**   if r = 100.54 **45.7**

2. Solve w + 23.65
if w = 21.35 **45**   if w = 45.77 **69.42**   if w = 0.899 **24.549**

Bonus Box: Four mugs are sold for $3.00. How many mugs can you buy for $12.00? How much will 36 mugs cost? 16 for 72¢   36 for 27¢

Page 84

▲ Find the products. Simplify to lowest terms.

1. $\frac{2}{3} \times \frac{9}{10} = \frac{3}{5}$ 2. $\frac{5}{6} \times \frac{3}{10} = \frac{1}{4}$ 3. $\frac{2}{5} \times \frac{10}{11} = \frac{4}{11}$

4. $\frac{4}{9} \times \frac{6}{7} = \frac{8}{21}$ 5. $\frac{1}{12} \times \frac{3}{4} = \frac{1}{16}$ 6. $\frac{1}{7} \times \frac{2}{5} = \frac{2}{35}$

▲ Refer to the table to calculate the relative frequency of each event. Write as a ratio.

Favorite Writing Tools

Grade	Pens	Pencils	Markers	Colored Pencils
Fifth	36	52	22	10
Sixth	41	53	11	25
Seventh	63	65	20	12

What is the relative frequency of a . . .

1. seventh grader preferring markers? **20:166**
2. fifth or sixth grader preferring pencils? **105:250**
3. fifth grader preferring pencils or pens? **88:120**
4. fifth or seventh grader preferring pens or markers? **135:290**
5. sixth grader preferring markers or colored pencils? **36:130**
6. fifth, sixth, or seventh grader preferring pens? **140:410**

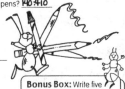

▲ Solve each algebraic expression for the given values.

1. $79.2 + u =$ **80.07**
   $u = 0.87$
2. $8a =$ **20.8**
   $a = 2.6$
3. $3\frac{5}{6} + n =$ **5½**
   $n = 1\frac{2}{3}$
4. $y/9 =$ **4.5**
   $y = 40.5$

Bonus Box: Write five number sentences with an answer of −4. **Answers will vary.**

Page 84

Page 85

▲ Find the products. Simplify to lowest terms.

1. $3 \times \frac{2}{3} =$ **2**   2. $\frac{4}{5} \times \frac{1}{3} = \frac{4}{15}$ 3. $\frac{3}{7} \times 2 = \frac{6}{7}$

4. $\frac{24}{25} \times \frac{5}{8} = \frac{3}{5}$ 5. $8 \times \frac{3}{8} =$ **3**   6. $\frac{3}{4} \times \frac{10}{12} = \frac{5}{8}$

▲ Refer to the table to calculate the probability of each event. Write as a ratio.

Study Time Preferences at Lakeshore School

Grade	Before School	Study Hall	After School	Evening
Fifth	16	82	51	41
Sixth	29	55	54	62
Seventh	31	84	42	53

What is the probability that a . . .

1. sixth grader prefers studying before school? **29:200**
2. sixth or seventh grader prefers studying in study hall? **139:410**
3. fifth grader prefers studying in the evening? **41:190**
4. fifth or seventh grader prefers studying after school? **93:400**
5. seventh grader prefers studying after school or in the evening? **95:210**
6. fifth, sixth, or seventh grader prefers studying before school or in the evening? **232:600**

▲ Solve each algebraic expression for the given values.

1. $k + \frac{4}{5} =$ **1 7/15**
   $k = \frac{2}{3}$
2. $9/p =$ **.2**
   $p = 45$
3. $z - 2\frac{3}{4} =$ **3 3/8**
   $z = 6\frac{1}{8}$
4. $2t =$ **1 4/5**
   $t = \frac{9}{10}$

Bonus Box: Use the data in the table above to write five probability statements with answers. **AWV**

Page 85

Page 86

▲ Find the products. Simplify to lowest terms.

1. $\frac{1}{4} \times 2 = \frac{1}{2}$ 2. $\frac{2}{5} \times \frac{5}{6} = \frac{1}{3}$ 3. $\frac{4}{7} \times \frac{3}{8} = \frac{3}{14}$

4. $\frac{3}{4} \times \frac{1}{2} = \frac{3}{8}$ 5. $\frac{14}{21} \times \frac{7}{14} = \frac{1}{3}$ 6. $\frac{2}{3} \times \frac{5}{8} = \frac{5}{12}$

▲ Refer to the tree diagrams of possible combinations of doughnut topping choices.

chocolate frosting — plain / sprinkles / coconut / nuts   vanilla frosting — plain / sprinkles / coconut / nuts

What is the probability of having a doughnut with . . .

1. chocolate frosting and nuts? **1:8**
2. plain frosting? **2:8**
3. frosting with sprinkles? **2:8**
4. chocolate frosting and coconut or nuts? **2:8**
5. vanilla frosting with coconut, nuts, or sprinkles? **3:8**
6. cherry frosting with sprinkles? **0:8**

▲ Solve each algebraic expression for the given values.

1. $4.2b =$ **23.814**
   $b = 5.67$
2. $\frac{1}{3} + s =$ **1 1/12**
   $s = \frac{3}{4}$
3. $w0.23 =$ **4**
   $w = 0.92$
4. $2\frac{4}{5} - k =$ **1 7/10**
   $k = \frac{11}{10}$

Bonus Box: Six doughnuts sell for $1.50. How many doughnuts can you buy for $9.00? How much will four dozen doughnuts cost? **36 for $9.00 4 doz = $12.00**

Page 86

Page 87

▲ Find the quotients. Simplify to lowest terms. The first one is done for you.

1. $\frac{1}{2} \div \frac{3}{4} = \frac{1}{2} \times \frac{4}{3} = \frac{4}{6} = \frac{2}{3}$
2. $\frac{3}{5} \div \frac{6}{7} =$ **7/10**
3. $\frac{2}{9} \div \frac{4}{6} =$ **2/6 or 1/3**
4. $\frac{1}{10} \div \frac{2}{5} =$ **1/4**

▲ Draw tree diagrams to illustrate possible combinations of two chores at Sally's house.

Choose one dinner chore: Choose one cleaning chore:
wash dishes   vacuum
dry dishes   dust
set table   sweep
clear table   windows

wash — vac. / dust / sweep / win.   set — vac. / dust / sweep / win.
dry — vac. / dust / sweep / win.   clear — vac. / dust / sweep / win.

What is the probability of choosing . . .

1. to wash dishes and dust or vacuum? **2:16**
2. to set or clear the table and vacuum or sweep? **4:16**
3. to wash the windows? **4:16**
4. to set the table? **4:16**
5. to set the table and dust or do windows? **2:16**
6. wash or dry dishes and sweep? **2:16**

▲ Solve for each letter.

1. $h - \frac{5}{6} = 1\frac{1}{3}$
   $h =$ **2 1/6**
2. $3.5 - p = 1.017$
   $p =$ **2.483**
3. $s/4 = 62$
   $s =$ **248**
4. $\frac{1}{2}n = \frac{2}{5}$
   $n =$ **4/5**

Bonus Box: Write five numbers that have 9 digits each so that the sum of the digits for each number is 46, and the first digit is equal to the last digit. **AWV**

Page 87

124

Page 88

Name _____

▲ Find the quotients. Simplify to lowest terms.

1. $\frac{4}{5} \div \frac{2}{7} = 2\,4/5$
2. $\frac{1}{9} \div \frac{5}{6} = 2/15$
3. $\frac{2}{9} \div \frac{1}{12} = 2\,2/3$
4. $\frac{3}{10} \div \frac{9}{14} = 7/15$
5. $\frac{1}{2} \div \frac{7}{8} = 4/7$
6. $\frac{4}{7} \div \frac{2}{3} = 6/7$

▲ Draw tree diagrams to illustrate the possible combinations of project choices. Each student must make one choice from each column.

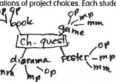

What is the probability of choosing . . .

1. the written report? 1:24
2. the game? 6:24
3. the oral presentation? 8:24
4. the chapter questions and a movement presentation? 4:24
5. the diorama and a multi-media presentation? 2:24
6. the written report, a book, and an oral presentation? 1:24

▲ Solve for each letter.

1. $\frac{2}{5} + g = \frac{7}{10}$; g = 4/7
2. r − 1,463 = 837 ; r = 2,300
3. e/2.2 = 89.1 ; e = 196.02
4. b0.62 = 26.598 ; b = 42.9
5. $\frac{2}{3} + c + \frac{4}{9} = 1\frac{5}{18}$; c = 1/6
6. $4\frac{1}{2} - f = 3\frac{1}{8}$; f = 1 3/8

Bonus Box: Sketch four rectangles. Label the length of each side. Find the perimeter and area of each figure. AWV

Page 89

Name _____

▲ Find the quotients. Simplify to lowest terms.

1. $\frac{4}{9} \div \frac{12}{27} = 1$
2. $\frac{5}{12} \div \frac{1}{6} = 2\frac{1}{2}$
3. $\frac{2}{7} \div \frac{4}{9} = \frac{9}{14}$
4. $\frac{2}{3} \div \frac{4}{9} = 1\frac{1}{2}$
5. $\frac{7}{10} \div \frac{3}{5} = 1\frac{1}{6}$
6. $\frac{1}{8} \div \frac{3}{4} = \frac{1}{6}$

▲ There are 5 blue cubes, 8 purple cubes, and 7 white cubes in a box. Write the probability of choosing . . .

1. a blue cube. 5:20
2. a red cube. 0:20
3. a purple marble. 0:20
4. a purple cube. 8:20
5. a white cube. 7:20

If you return the cube to the bag each time, what is the probability of choosing . . .

1. a white cube if you make 100 picks? 35:100
2. a blue or purple cube if you make 40 picks? 26:40

▲ Solve for each letter.

1. 3.06 + m = 39.682 = 67.213   m = 24.471
2. .09s = 3.852   s = 42.8
3. k − 1.6429 = 0.4571   k = 2.1
4. 325.89/p = 5.1   p = 63.9
5. 1 + 274,809 = 744,047   t = 469,238
6. 8.3a = 18.758   a = 2.26

Bonus Box: Show at least 5 ways to make $2.61 using coins. AWV

Page 90

Name _____

▲ Find the quotients. Simplify to lowest terms.

1. $\frac{6}{7} \div \frac{2}{3} = 1\,2/7$
2. $\frac{5}{9} \div \frac{7}{12} = 20/21$
3. $\frac{4}{7} \div \frac{2}{5} = 1\,3/7$
4. $\frac{3}{4} \div \frac{15}{16} = 4/5$
5. $\frac{1}{9} \div \frac{2}{15} = 5/6$
6. $\frac{9}{10} \div \frac{12}{15} = 1\,1/8$

▲ There are 3 hot-pink sunglasses, 15 navy blue sunglasses, 12 cherry-red sunglasses, and 8 sunshine-yellow sunglasses in a box. What is the probability of choosing . . .

1. navy blue sunglasses? 15:38
2. cherry-red or sunshine-yellow sunglasses? 20:38
3. forest-green sunglasses? 0:38
4. hot-pink sunglasses? 3:38
5. sunshine-yellow, hot-pink, or navy blue sunglasses? 26:38

If you return the sunglasses to the box each time, what is the probability of choosing . . .

1. hot-pink sunglasses if you make 228 picks? 18:228
2. navy blue or cherry-red sunglasses if you make 152 picks? 108:152

▲ Solve for each letter.

s = (m + n) (j − k)
m + m = j
n + n = m
n + k = 5
k − n = 1
s = 30   m = 4   n = 2
j = 8   k = 3

Bonus Box: Find and trace twelve angles. Find three obtuse angles, three right angles, and three acute angles. Label each and write where you found each. AWV

Page 91

Name _____

▲ Multiply or divide. Simplify to lowest terms.

1. $\frac{4}{5} \times \frac{1}{6} = \frac{2}{15}$
2. $\frac{8}{9} \times \frac{3}{7} = \frac{8}{21}$
3. $\frac{14}{25} \times \frac{5}{7} = \frac{2}{5}$
4. $\frac{2}{3} \div \frac{4}{9} = 1\frac{1}{2}$
5. $\frac{3}{4} \div \frac{9}{10} = \frac{5}{6}$
6. $\frac{7}{8} \div \frac{1}{4} = 3\frac{1}{2}$

▲ There are 12 mint, 15 toffee, 10 caramel, and 14 chocolate candies in a bag. What is the probability of choosing . . .

1. a mint candy? 12:51
2. a chocolate candy? 14:51
3. a toffee or caramel candy? 25:51
4. a coconut candy? 0:51
5. a mint, chocolate, or toffee candy? 41:51

If you return the candy to the box each time, what is the probability of choosing . . .

1. a caramel candy if you make 357 picks? 70:357
2. a chocolate or caramel candy if you make 152 picks? 72:152

▲ Solve for each letter.

b + c = d + c + e − 9
c + 1 = d
2d = e
e − b = c
c − 3 = 8 − 7
b = 6   c = 4   d = 5
e = 10

24oz for 21q.
16oz. for 12q. of water.

Bonus Box: Four ounces of cleaner is needed for three quarts of water. How many ounces of cleaner are needed for twenty-one quarts of water? How much water is needed for 16 ounces of cleaner?

Page 92

▲ Multiply. Simplify to lowest terms. The first one is done for you.

1. $3 \times \frac{4}{3} = \frac{12}{3}$ or **4**

2. $\frac{5}{8} \times 12 = 7\frac{1}{2}$

3. $\frac{4}{5} \times 10 = 8$

4. $6 \times \frac{1}{4} = 1\frac{1}{2}$

5. $\frac{5}{6} \times 8 = 6\frac{2}{3}$

6. $3 \times \frac{4}{9} = 1\frac{1}{3}$

▲ Use the spinner to determine the probability of each event.

What is the probability of the spinner . . .

1. stopping on an 8? **1:8**
2. stopping on a number less than 14? **6:8**
3. stopping on a number greater than or equal to 6? **6:8**
4. stopping on an even number? **8:8**
5. stopping on an odd number? **0:8**
6. stopping on 6, 8, 10, 14, or 16? **5:8**

(spinner showing 16, 2, 14, 4, 12, 6, 10, 8)

▲ Room 34 recorded on a stem-and-leaf plot the passing scores for a science project. Use the stem-and-leaf plot to answer the questions.

Passing Scores

9	0 0 2 3 4 7 8
8	0 0 1 1 1 1 5 7 7 7 9
7	4 6 7 7 8 9
6	7 8 9 9

1. Which score occurred most often? **81**
2. How many students had passing scores? **28**
3. If there are 35 people in the class, how many students did not have a passing grade? **7**
4. A score of 78 to 86 is a "B." How many students received a "B"? **9**
5. What is the probability that Cia earned a "B" for her project grade? **9:35**

Bonus Box: Write five numbers with ten digits each so that the sum of the digits for each number is less than thirty, and the digit in the tenths place is four. **AWV**

Page 92

Page 93

▲ Multiply. Simplify to lowest terms. The first one is done for you.

1. $5\frac{1}{4} \times 2\frac{2}{7} = $ **12**

2. $1\frac{7}{9} \times 4\frac{1}{2} = 8$

3. $3\frac{1}{3} \times 1\frac{1}{2} = 5$

4. $3\frac{3}{5} \times \frac{2}{9} = \frac{4}{5}$

5. $1\frac{5}{7} \times \frac{5}{6} = 1\frac{3}{7}$

6. $\frac{3}{7} \times 5\frac{1}{4} = 2\frac{1}{4}$

▲ Match the words with the definitions.

c 1. acute triangle — a. a closed figure with three sides and three vertices

e 2. octagon — b. a quadrilateral with one set of parallel sides

a 3. triangle — c. a triangle with one angle that is less than 90°

b 4. trapezoid — d. a quadrilateral with opposite sides that are parallel

d 5. parallelogram — e. a polygon with 8 sides and 8 vertices

▲ For three weeks, William recorded his heart rate after running one mile. Use the stem-and-leaf plot to answer the questions.

Heart rate

17	0 2 2 3 4 4 5 7
16	3 5 5 5 5 7 8
15	1 3 8 8 9

1. Which heart rate occurred most often? **165**
2. What are the heart rates shown by the first stem and its leaves? **170, 172, 172, 173, 174, 174, 175, 177**
3. What is the mode? **165**
4. What is the median heart rate? **166**
5. Which heart rate occurred more often, 158 or 167? **158**

Bonus Box: Use the data in the stem-and-leaf plot to make a bar graph. **Answers will vary.**

Page 93

Page 94

▲ Multiply. Reduce to lowest terms.

1. $3\frac{1}{3} \times 2\frac{1}{4} = 7\frac{1}{2}$

2. $2\frac{2}{5} \times \frac{2}{9} = \frac{8}{15}$

3. $6\frac{2}{3} \times 2\frac{1}{4} = 15$

4. $2\frac{3}{4} \times 2\frac{2}{3} = 7\frac{1}{3}$

5. $2\frac{1}{7} \times 2\frac{4}{5} = 6$

6. $10\frac{1}{2} \times 3\frac{1}{3} = 35$

▲ Match the words with the definitions.

c 1. quadrilateral — a. a polygon with 6 sides and 6 vertices

b 2. right triangle — b. a triangle with one 90° angle

a 3. hexagon — c. a polygon with 4 sides and 4 vertices

e 4. pentagon — d. a triangle with one angle that is greater than 90°

d 5. obtuse triangle — e. a polygon with 5 sides and 5 vertices

▲ Use the following data to make a stem-and-leaf plot. Then use the stem-and-leaf plot to answer the questions.

Data

18	10	24	30	41	42
31	18	27	33	40	43
27	37	15	39	27	43
17	36	26	16	41	40

Numbers

4	0011233
3	013679
2	46777
1	056788

1. What numbers are shown by the first stem and its leaves? **40, 40, 41, 41, 42, 43, 43**
2. What is the mode? **27**
3. What is the median? **30**
4. What is the range? **33**

Bonus Box: Sketch each of the geometric figures described above.

Page 94

Page 95

▲ Multiply. Simplify to lowest terms.

1. $5\frac{2}{6} \times 2\frac{2}{8} = 13\frac{7}{9}$

2. $4\frac{6}{9} \times 6\frac{3}{4} = 31\frac{1}{2}$

3. $5\frac{1}{3} \times \frac{1}{16} = \frac{1}{3}$

4. $3\frac{1}{3} \times 2\frac{1}{4} = 7\frac{1}{2}$

5. $2\frac{2}{9} \times 1\frac{1}{5} = 2\frac{2}{3}$

6. $2\frac{3}{6} \times \frac{9}{10} = 2\frac{1}{4}$

▲ Write the numeral for each number word.

1. Seven billion, ten thousand, four and six tenths **7,000,010,004.6**
2. Fifty-eight million, two hundred thousand, sixty-five and fifteen hundredths **58,200,065.15**
3. Seventy-nine and five thousandths **79.005**
4. Nine hundred sixty-one billion, one hundred million, seven hundred twenty-four **961,100,000,724**
5. Six and forty-five ten thousandths **6.0045**

▲ Add or subtract.

1.
$$50,000,000 - 23,089,702 = 26,910,298$$

2.
$$400,000 - 39,002 = 360,998$$

3.
$$56,873,298 + 25,361,345 = 82,234,643$$

4.
$$90,003,000 - 21,345,321 = 68,657,679$$

Bonus Box: Fifteen coins are in a bank. One-fifth are dimes, and one-third are quarters. There are no pennies. What could be the value of the coins in the bank? Provide two possibilities. **Answers will vary.**

Page 95

126

© Carson-Dellosa   IF87123 • Mixed Skills in Math 5-6

Page 96

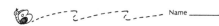

▲ Divide. Simplify to lowest terms.

1. $4 \frac{2}{3} \div \frac{8}{9} = 5\frac{1}{4}$ 2. $3 \frac{3}{6} \div 4 \frac{2}{3} = \frac{3}{4}$ 3. $1 \frac{1}{7} \div 1 \frac{3}{7} = \frac{4}{5}$

4. $1 \frac{7}{8} \div 7 \frac{2}{4} = \frac{1}{4}$ 5. $1 \frac{5}{9} \div 3 \frac{1}{3} = \frac{7}{15}$ 6. $3 \frac{9}{10} \div 1 \frac{4}{5} = 2\frac{1}{6}$

▲ Round . . .

1. to the nearest hundred thousand.

456,736,225,142 → 456,736,200,000
56,950,382,001 → 56,950,400,000
156,723,645.2573 → 156,700,000

2. to the nearest hundredth.

352,637.84328 → 352,637.84
10.08923 → 10.09
9,452.367 1623 → 9,452,367.16

3. to the nearest ten million.

34,526,738,901.223 → 34,530,000,000
245,174,838.5562 → 250,000,000
321,234,683 → 320,000,000

▲ Add.

1.
8,352,716
1,023,637
425,673
2,115
+ 41
9,804,182

2.
601,231
235,637
24,601
34,256
+ 1,617
897,342

3.
1,002,573
4,341,734
83,261
5,372
+ 709
5,433,649

Bonus Box: Write four numbers that when rounded to the nearest ten thousand, round to 432,156,280,000. Include numbers that round up and numbers that round down. Answers will vary.

Page 97

▲ Divide. Simplify to lowest terms.

1. $2 \frac{2}{8} \div 6 \frac{3}{4} = \frac{1}{3}$ 2. $5 \frac{5}{8} \div 2 \frac{3}{16} = 2\frac{4}{7}$ 3. $6 \frac{2}{9} \div 3 \frac{3}{6} = 1\frac{7}{9}$

4. $7 \frac{1}{5} \div 30 = \frac{6}{25}$ 5. $2 \frac{3}{6} \div 2 \frac{2}{9} = 1\frac{1}{8}$ 6. $2 \frac{4}{5} \div 2 \frac{1}{10} = 1\frac{1}{3}$

▲ Find the perimeter of each figure.

1. 19cm, 10cm, 14cm, 12cm, 29cm → 84 cm
2. 63 in., 28 in. → 182 in.
3. 4m, 5m, 7m → 16 m

▲ Multiply or divide.

1. 623 × 54 = 33,642
2. 47|18,706 = 398
3. 73|67,671 = 927
4. 296 × 37 = 10,952
5. 61|34,953 = 573
6. 28|19,460 = 695

Bonus Box: Use grid paper to sketch five different shapes with an area of 22 square units. Find the perimeter of each. AWV

Page 98

▲ Divide. Simplify to lowest terms.

1. $1 \frac{7}{15} \div 2 \frac{4}{5} = \frac{11}{21}$ 2. $1 \frac{13}{14} \div 1 \frac{5}{7} = 1\frac{1}{8}$ 3. $1 \frac{7}{8} \div \frac{9}{32} = 6\frac{2}{3}$

4. $3 \frac{3}{14} \div 2 \frac{4}{7} = 1\frac{1}{4}$ 5. $3 \frac{3}{6} \div 5 \frac{5}{6} = \frac{3}{5}$ 6. $2 \frac{6}{7} \div 2 \frac{2}{14} = 1\frac{1}{3}$

▲ Use the correct order of operations.

1. $(2 - 1) \times (3 + 6) = 9$
2. $(46 - 6) + (2 + 1 \times 2) = 10$
3. $21 \div 7 + (2 + 6) \times 4 = 35$
4. $(2 + 10 - 3) + (1 + 2) = 3$
5. $(6 + 24 \div 6) \div 5 = 2$
6. $10 \times 6 \div (3 + 5 + 2) = 6$

▲ Add or subtract.

1.
4.28998
31.4972
+ 0.19213
35.97931

2.
53.67
− 49.25734
4.41266

3.
9.004
− 5.83241
3.17159

4.
63.208
412.52
+ 98.3522
574.0802

Bonus Box: Change problem number 2 from the order of operations activity to equal 45. Change number 2 to equal 42.
*2. $46 - 6 \div 2 + 1 \times 2 = 45$
$46 - 6 \div (2 + 1) \times 2 = 42$

Page 99

▲ Divide. Simplify to lowest terms.

1. $2 \frac{4}{5} \div 2 \frac{1}{10} = 1\frac{1}{3}$ 2. $1 \frac{1}{3} \div 1 \frac{13}{27} = \frac{9}{10}$ 3. $3 \frac{3}{4} \div 1 \frac{7}{18} = 2\frac{7}{10}$

4. $3 \frac{1}{3} \div \frac{14}{27} = 6\frac{3}{7}$ 5. $3 \frac{3}{5} \div 1 \frac{1}{15} = 3\frac{3}{8}$ 6. $1 \frac{1}{5} \div 2 \frac{2}{5} = \frac{1}{2}$

▲ Find the mean, mode, median, and range for each set of numbers. Complete the chart.

Set A: 5 7 5 9 6 5 5 8 4
Set B: 26 30 42 55 63 50
Set C: 2 93 46 4 16 4 99

Set	Mean	Mode	Median	Range
A	6	5	5	5
B	44.3	None	46	37
C	37.7	4	16	97

▲ Multiply or divide.

1. .018|5.274 = 293
2. .74|11.988 = 16.2
3. 98.2 × 7.8 = 765.96
4. 42.9 × 6.2 = 265.98

Bonus Box: You can buy four tadpoles for $0.66. How many tadpoles can you get for $4.62? 28 How much will 36 tadpoles cost? $5.94

Page 100

Name _____

▲ Multiply or divide. Simplify to lowest terms.

1. $1\frac{1}{15} + 2\frac{2}{3} = \frac{2}{5}$
2. $1\frac{1}{14} \times 2\frac{1}{10} = 2\frac{1}{4}$
3. $2\frac{12}{15} \div 7\frac{1}{5} = \frac{7}{18}$
4. $3\frac{3}{4} \times 1\frac{1}{5} = 4\frac{1}{2}$
5. $1\frac{1}{5} \times 1\frac{3}{12} = 1\frac{1}{2}$
6. $\frac{8}{21} \div 1\frac{5}{7} = \frac{2}{9}$

▲ Write each decimal. Change each decimal to a percent. Change the percents to fractions. Write the fractions in lowest terms.

	Decimal	Percent	Fraction
1. twenty hundredths	.20	20%	$\frac{1}{5}$
2. fifty-five hundredths	.55	55%	$\frac{11}{20}$
3. thirty-eight hundredths	.38	38%	$\frac{19}{50}$
4. eight hundredths	.08	8%	$\frac{2}{25}$
5. ninety-two hundredths	.92	92%	$\frac{23}{25}$
6. fifteen hundredths	.15	15%	$\frac{3}{20}$

▲ Add or subtract the integers.

1. $-7 - {}^+4 = -11$
2. $-3 + {}^-5 = -8$
3. $^+4 + {}^+7 = {}^+11$
4. $-7 + {}^-9 = -16$
5. $-16 - {}^+1 = -17$
6. $-14 - {}^-17 = {}^+3$
7. $^+2 + {}^-10 = -8$
8. $-12 + {}^+9 = -3$

Bonus Box: Write five number sentences with an answer of −8.

Page 100

Page 101

Name _____

▲ Multiply and divide. Simplify to lowest terms.

1. $1\frac{1}{9} \div 1\frac{1}{3} = \frac{5}{6}$
2. $1\frac{1}{5} \div 2\frac{2}{5} = \frac{1}{2}$
3. $5\frac{1}{4} \times 1\frac{1}{7} = 6$
4. $2\frac{2}{5} \times 1\frac{1}{14} = 1\frac{4}{7}$
5. $2\frac{1}{7} \div 4\frac{2}{7} = \frac{1}{2}$
6. $1\frac{1}{9} \div \frac{1}{9} = 10$

▲ Refer to the table to calculate the relative frequency of each event. Write as a ratio.

Seventh-Hour Class Choices

Grade	Rockets	Chemistry	Drama	Sculpture
Fifth	25	28	22	30
Sixth	34	26	45	15
Seventh	52	39	8	31

What is the relative frequency of a . . .

1. seventh grader taking drama? 8:130
2. fifth or sixth grader taking rockets? 59:225
3. fifth grader taking rockets or chemistry? 53:105
4. sixth or seventh grader taking drama or chemistry? 118:250
5. sixth grader taking drama or sculpture? 60:120
6. fifth, sixth, or seventh grader taking chemistry? 93:335

▲ Solve each algebraic expression for the given values.

1. $6.2 + k = $ 11.17
   k = 4.97
2. $\frac{1}{3}s = $ 4
   s = 12
3. $3\frac{1}{3} - p = $ 1$\frac{2}{3}$
   p = 1$\frac{2}{3}$

Bonus Box: Write five numbers that have ten digits each so that each number has the digit 5 in the hundredths place, and the sum of the digits is 66. **Answers will vary.**

Page 101

Page 102

Name _____

▲ Multiply and divide. Simplify to lowest terms.

1. $1\frac{3}{4} \div 3\frac{1}{2} = \frac{1}{2}$
2. $5\frac{5}{6} \times \frac{3}{10} = 1\frac{3}{4}$
3. $4\frac{4}{5} \div 1\frac{1}{15} = 4\frac{1}{2}$
4. $2\frac{4}{7} \times 2\frac{3}{9} = 6$
5. $\frac{13}{16} \times 2\frac{2}{3} = 2\frac{1}{6}$
6. $1\frac{1}{2} \div 2\frac{2}{11} = \frac{11}{16}$

▲ Draw tree diagrams to illustrate the possible combinations of snack and beverage choices.

Choose one beverage: hot chocolate, pop, fruit juice, water

Choose one snack: pie, cake, cookies, fruit

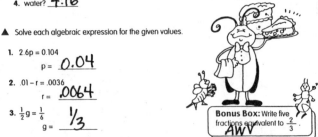

What is the probability of having . . .

1. hot chocolate and pie? 1:16
2. fruit juice or pop with cookies? 2:16
3. cake? 4:16
4. water? 4:16
5. water and pie, cake, or cookies? 3:16
6. hot chocolate or fruit juice with cookies, cake, or fruit? 6:16

▲ Solve each algebraic expression for the given values.

1. $2.6p = 0.104$
   p = 0.04
2. $.01 - r = .0036$
   r = .0064
3. $\frac{1}{2}g = \frac{1}{6}$
   g = $\frac{1}{3}$

Bonus Box: Write five fractions equivalent to $\frac{2}{3}$. AWV

Page 102

Page 103

Name _____

▲ Solve. Simplify to lowest terms.

1. $7\frac{1}{5} + 1\frac{1}{5} = 6$
2. $3\frac{1}{3} - 2\frac{2}{3} = \frac{2}{3}$
3. $3\frac{3}{4} \times 1\frac{1}{5} = 4\frac{1}{2}$
4. $2\frac{3}{4} + 4\frac{3}{4} = 7\frac{1}{2}$
5. $9\frac{1}{5} - 2\frac{3}{5} = 6\frac{3}{5}$
6. $2\frac{1}{10} + 2\frac{4}{5} = \frac{3}{4}$

▲ Solve for each letter.

1. a = (b − t) x a + t
   a + t = 3
   t + t + t = a
   t < 3
   3 < a < 8
   a = 6 b = 4 t = 2

2. s + (p − r) − (m x c) = c
   c + c = m
   m + m = p
   1 + r = p
   p + c = s
   3c = 6
   c = 2 m = 4 p = 8 r = 7 s = 10

▲ Refer to the stem-and-leaf plot to answer the questions.

Numbers

7	3 3 5 6 7 7 9
6	2 4 5 5 6 8 9 9
5	0 1 2 2 5 7 8
4	0 1 1 1 5 8

1. What is the range? 39
2. Which number occurred most often? 41
3. What numbers are shown in the fourth leaf? 40,41,41,41,45,48
4. What is the mode? 41
5. What is the median? 64

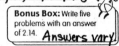

Bonus Box: Write five problems with an answer of 2.14. **Answers vary.**

Page 103